250 RULES *of* BUSINESS

Steven Schragis is one of the smartest guys I know. When it comes to business, he knows every angle—including what to say and how to say it!

—Donald Trump

Rick is my go-to guy for book publicity and marketing. I trust him deeply and he's earned his reputation as an expert, a creative confidante, and the best book publicist in the nation.

—Brendon Burchard, Author, *THE CHARGE*, and
The Millionaire Messenger, Founder, High
Performance Academy and Experts Academy

There are only ten people who understand and have mastered the book publishing process—Rick Frishman is one of them—I have counseled him, listened to him, and watched the books he promoted turn to gold. If you're looking for someone to take your book to the promised land, I promise that Rick Frishman is the rocket ship that will take you there.

—Jeffrey Gitomer, Founding Partner at Ace of Sales

250 RULES of BUSINESS

Secrets to Growing Your Career and Profits

Steven Schragis and Rick Frishman

NEW YORK

250 RULES of BUSINESS
Secrets to Growing Your Career and Profits

ISBN 978-1-61448-516-2 paperback
ISBN 978-1-61448-517-9 eBook
Library of Congress Control Number: 2013933692

Morgan James Publishing
The Entrepreneurial Publisher
5 Penn Plaza, 23rd Floor,
New York City, New York 10001
(212) 655-5470 office • (516) 908-4496 fax
www.MorganJamesPublishing.com

Cover Design by:
Rachel Lopez
www.r2cdesign.com

Interior Design by:
Bonnie Bushman
bonnie@caboodlegraphics.com

In an effort to support local communities, raise awareness and funds, Morgan James Publishing donates a percentage of all book sales for the life of each book to Habitat for Humanity Peninsula and Greater Williamsburg.

Get involved today, visit
www.MorganJamesBuilds.com.

Habitat
for Humanity®
Peninsula and
Greater Williamsburg
Building Partner

To my wife Donna,
this book could never have been written
without your love and encouragement
STEVEN SCHRAGIS

To my wife Robbi, with love and thanks
RICK FRISHMAN

INTRODUCTION

Starting, managing and growing a business isn't easy, and everyone is quick to offer you differing advice. Thousands of business books, articles, programs, courses, and workshops insist that they have the answers. Many of them are superficial, theoretical, impractical, or unclear, and they often contradict each. It all gets confusing and you don't know where to turn.

Over the years, we've had the good fortune to meet, work with, and spend considerable time with many highly respected and successful business leaders. These individuals have worked in the trenches, solved the hard problems, rallied the troops, and risen to the top of their fields where they harvested record profits. Many of these leaders have become our teachers, mentors, colleagues, and friends. We've watched them operate, conducted business with them, and benefited from their advice.

We made it our practice to ask them to share a single business insight with us—a basic rule, practice, or belief that played an important role in their success. Some of the responses we received were basic, intuitive, and items that we already knew. But others were amazing and eye opening; they constantly made us stop and think.

The point is, as Yogi Berra said, you can observe a lot by just watching. So we wrote them down and spent time examining if and how they could work for us. Then we tried to apply them to our businesses, careers, and other aspects of our lives.

Steven Schragis
Rick Frishman

The
Rules

DON'T MAKE
RUSHED DECISIONS

If the issue is serious, never make a decision on the spot unless you absolutely have to. Think it over for a few minutes, an evening, or a weekend, and then go into the office with your answer. Give yourself the time you need to avoid the mistakes that often result from haste.

WHAT IT MEANS: Clearly, decisions can vary considerably in their urgency, importance, and complexity—and so no one rule of thumb fits all—but you should never be pressured into giving a quick yes or no before you've given yourself adequate time to think it through. At the end of the day, it's much more about the quality of your decisions than the time it took to make them.

ACTION PLAN: Make it a point to never make an instant decision if there isn't a compelling reason to do so. Make sure you have the facts. And then go grab a cup of coffee or take a walk around the block or resolve to sleep on it. More often than not, you have the right to give yourself a little time to breathe—and think it over.

EVEN BETTER: Write it down! List the pros and cons of making your decision one way or another. Listing and evaluating the relevant considerations and potential consequences can be a very useful tool for helping you to think things through. And the very process itself can be a healthy brake on the tendency to make snap decisions.

RULE TWO
UNDERPROMISE AND OVERDELIVER

This is the one thing you can always do to improve business relationships and reinforce your reputation for reliability: Deliver what you promise. In fact, you should even take it one step further. If at all possible, strive to deliver a little more than promised—or a day or two ahead of schedule. When it comes to being perceived as a reliable professional, there is no margin of error for keeping your word.

WHAT IT MEANS: It's all about managing expectations. Whenever you make a promise, you have stated your commitment to perform something. As a result, you have created a certain level of expectation—and by scaling down this expectation, you can more easily create a positive outcome. Remember, when you provide more than what was expected by your customer, you enhance any good feelings they already have about you.

ACTION PLAN: Before you make any sort of promise, carefully think through everything you'll need to do to deliver properly within the time frame you've created. Avoid the natural tendency to say yes to everything. If you make ten promises and fail to deliver just once, people are not going to remember your nine successes.

EVEN BETTER: When you think you're done, and that you've kept your promise as well as you possibly can, don't stop. Try and think of what you can do to do even better. Perhaps you'll have some ideas that you hadn't thought of earlier. Developing a reputation as someone who exceeds expectations is invaluable.

RULE THREE
RELEARN THE
ENGLISH LANGUAGE

When you're dealing with people in your industry or profession, there are certain buzzwords and jargon that everyone knows and understands, and there's no problem in using them. This puts you on the same page as everyone else, and it even helps reinforce relationships between industry insiders. After a while, however, everyone gets tired of jargon and buzzwords. It doesn't matter whether you're an industry insider or not, there comes a point where you just get tired of it all and want to speak and be spoken to in plain, straightforward language.

WHAT IT MEANS: In business, you've always got to know whom you're talking to, and then use the right level of industry jargon. Not too much … not too little. When speaking to industry outsiders, make sure you're not talking over their heads. If you edit your written and spoken communications, you will have a better chance of establishing and maintaining a strong relationship.

ACTION PLAN: Use analogies or plain English translations. People often understand complex messages if they are wrapped in analogies; the more universal the analogy, the better. Relating a concept to a trip to the grocery store, the car dealership, or a lemonade stand may seem simplistic, but these are activities that everyone has experienced.

EVEN BETTER: Pay careful attention to nonverbal cues as they will give you clues on what's difficult to grasp and requires more explanation. If your speech patterns are sprinkled with technical words without any corresponding explanation, chances are your listener's eyes will eventually glaze over. Adjust the level of industry language that you are using, both to make it easier to understand and to prompt questions when necessary.

RULE FOUR
WHEN THE SEASON
IS RIGHT, PLAY SANTA

Everyone likes getting gifts, even if they're too polite to say otherwise. Business gift giving is its own kind of art, but it is an art that you would do well to master. But remember: the best business gifts don't cost a lot, but they mean a lot.

Overly expensive and ostentatious gifts are never a good idea. Most companies have rules against that kind of thing—and even if they don't, such a gift will probably result in more discomfort and embarrassment than any genuine sense of appreciation.

WHAT IT MEANS: Don't give gifts too often—less is definitely more in this area—but the right gift, whether as a holiday-season thank-you or an unexpected little surprise is a great way to create more favorable impressions and more cordial relationships with clients and other key business contacts. So, give thoughtfully, appropriately, creatively, and personally.

ACTION PLAN: Whenever you read something that you think a business associate might benefit from, send a copy to that person with a short personal note. This may not be gift giving in the conventional sense at all, but it is certainly a thoughtful and effective token of appreciation.

EVEN BETTER: The very best gifts are generally gestures that acknowledge your appreciation of someone and your awareness of his or her interests. For example, a baseball souvenir for a true-blue Red Sox fan, or maybe some fine wool for an avid knitter. In a small but memorable way, these gifts say, "I was thinking about you, and I know you well enough to know that you would like this."

RULE FIVE
They Call It
Murphy's Law for a Reason

If something can go wrong, it will. There's a reason this axiom is called Murphy's Law, not Murphy's Reminder. So plan for the unexpected. Failing to plan realistically—overestimating sales; underestimating costs and time to market; and then failing to plan for the inevitable twists, bumps, and craters along the way—is the primary reason why most business start-ups fail. But even established companies tend to be far too rosy in their plans and forecasts and don't leave themselves a margin of error. If you're not willing to ground your plans in reality to make things appear to be better than they are, you're asking for trouble.

WHAT IT MEANS: In the real world, projects take longer and cost more than expected for all sorts of reasons. People get sick or quit. Shipments of critical components arrive late due to a natural disaster. A key supplier goes out of business. A last-minute technical glitch—one you or your team never anticipated—stops development dead in its tracks.

ACTION PLAN: Add some wiggle room to your budgets and project timelines. Chances are, you're going to need it. And if not, you will have pulled off a minor managerial miracle—a project that did even better than planned!

EVEN BETTER: Set up regular meetings to evaluate all aspects of major projects you're working on, and focus on what new developments have occurred. If you can use these meetings to forecast potential problems and keep them under control, you might be able to break Murphy's Law more than you'd expect.

RULE SIX
MONEY BUYS EVERYTHING, EXCEPT RESPECT

World famous management guru Tom Peters says it well: "Farmer, senator, salesperson, engineer, janitor, CEO, you, me, and the kid who mows your lawn—everybody loves being recognized, in any way, large or small."

Conversely, when you discount the value of your coworkers or employees by ignoring them, taking them for granted, or giving the impression that they are expendable and readily replaceable, they begin to act accordingly and become less valuable. It's a self-fulfilling prophecy. People start to unplug.

WHAT IT MEANS: Appreciation, applause, approval, respect—the fact is, people do not work for money alone. We appreciate being appreciated. And although a paycheck certainly is a tangible form of reward and recognition, the fact that it comes regularly often diminishes its motivational impact. Compared to the warmth of personal praise, paychecks are impersonal—and besides, everyone else is getting one! If you're criticizing or admonishing more than you're complimenting, you are heading down the wrong path.

ACTION PLAN: Smart managers know that the right words of praise or recognition at the right time can be worth their weight in gold. Actions that get rewarded, get repeated.

Try to catch people in the act of doing something right. And when you do, right then and there, tell them what you're thinking. Make every person feel like he or she really matters.

EVEN BETTER: Whenever you know you'll be with a group of your business associates, make it a point to think about and prepare some positive thoughts about others in the group—and then share them out loud. If there's anything people like more than praise, it's praise in front of others. You don't have to "get" everybody ... that's a bit too obvious. But over a period of time, no one should be left out.

RULE SEVEN
HIRE PEOPLE WHO DISAGREE WITH YOU

It's only human nature to be firmly attached to your own opinions, but that's not always the best way to manage. In fact, it almost never is. The opinions and perspectives of your coworkers and others may be an invaluable resource—yet it is often one that is undervalued and overlooked.

Diversity of thought won't always make it easier for you to make decisions. In fact, by pointing out possible pitfalls and gray areas, others may complicate certain decisions that initially seemed like no-brainers. But this practice will absolutely have a real positive impact on morale because everyone appreciates it when their opinions are sought, listened to, and valued.

WHAT IT MEANS: As a manager, you can gain the benefit of soliciting multiple viewpoints only if you actively and regularly send the signals that you welcome such feedback. Otherwise, people will be understandably reluctant to disagree. Ask people directly what they think of a particular strategy or proposal—and be sensitive to the fact that your feedback is more likely to be frank and uninhibited if it's sought in a one-on-one setting.

ACTION PLAN: Always make it a point to thank people who share their insights. And make it clear to everyone that they should always feel free to "weigh in" on a pending project or business decision if they have something to add to the discussion.

EVEN BETTER: Seeking input from people outside your immediate workgroup will help you to make smarter decisions, so be especially aggressive in seeking it out. Contact people you don't deal with on a regular basis and get their thoughts—great advice often comes from the most surprising places.

RULE EIGHT

If Technology's the Hare, then Employees Are the Tortoise

Regardless of any new technology that you might be considering, keep in mind that the most important part of a successful business is a persuaded and prepared employee. There is always a human component to the adaptation of any new technology—a component that many organizations do not consider as carefully as they should.

WHAT IT MEANS: New technology will do wonders for any organization—but you do need to give it time, and a little sensitivity and "hand holding" can make the transition easier and more effective. It's not just a question of learning which buttons to push—it's being aware of which "people buttons" not to push. Because we are all creatures of habit, there will always be resistance to new technologies, procedures, and processes—and even some fear and resentment.

ACTION PLAN: Breaking up training into more digestible chunks (instead of the typical and daunting marathon workshop) can help minimize the fear factor. Allow for practice, follow-up sessions, and individual instruction when needed. Accept the fact that there's a learning curve between being introduced to a new technology and becoming completely proficient.

EVEN BETTER: Don't be in a hurry to get a new system up and running ASAP. Make sure to give people enough time to fool around with it and get their feet wet. Allow a "new users group" to meet regularly to share their concerns and tips. Make the training more of an extended group experience, with mutual support and practice. Trial runs can help ease the resistance to new technologies and things.

Work *on* Your Business, Not Just *for* Your Business

There are many tasks that never "need to be done tomorrow." But they do, in fact, need to be done. Unless you regularly schedule time to work on growing your business and to answer critical questions, you may find yourself too busy to get to the issues you really need to focus on.

WHAT IT MEANS: Most businesspeople are so busy working for their business that they never find time to work on their business. But if you don't, who will? After all, many small-business owners spend virtually all of their time working, so they get kind of used to doing everything themselves. Putting out small or not-so-small fires and jumping around from task to task can keep you busy, and there's even something reassuring about it—you're within your comfort zone. But often it just isn't the best possible use of your time.

ACTION PLAN: Schedule some time regularly to do "big picture" stuff. Working on your business is about planning the future, planning management succession, selecting great employees, assigning and delegating tasks, considering new marketing strategies, securing new financing and/or equipment. Keep a list of things to do (and things you can do) to address these challenges—and keep doing them!

EVEN BETTER: Schedule a strategic retreat meeting with your senior management team. In a pleasant and secluded setting, away from the phones and minutia of daily business, you'll be more relaxed and prepared to focus in on one or more (fewer is better) critical business issues. Hire a consultant or corporate trainer to help facilitate group brainstorming.

RULE TEN

WITHOUT COMMUNICATION, YOU'RE DESTINED TO FAIL

I've heard that at least half of all management problems occur as a result of poor communication—and I believe it. As a business grows over time, the importance of maintaining and continually strengthening the level of communications throughout a company grows at an exponential rate.

WHAT IT MEANS: For almost any project or endeavor, snarls and snags are a fact of life. Deadlines don't always get met. Things fall between the cracks. People just don't get it. Good communications is the glue that can keep everyone in the organization more aware of what's really happening—or needs to happen—and why … and when! Timely and proactive information sharing is critical for running any organization more smoothly.

ACTION PLAN: Posting or e-mailing a weekly status report of all active projects—what's been done, what remains to be done, by when, and by whom—is a good way to get everyone you're working with on the same page.

EVEN BETTER: Always end your discussions by seeking and confirming clarification. It's better to ask a few "dumb" questions than to be misunderstood. Also, make it clear to subordinates exactly what you expect from them and when—and, if necessary, the relative priority of specific tasks. The less other people have to guess about what you expect, the fewer unpleasant surprises there will be.

COMPANIES DON'T HAVE PERSONALITIES—THEY HAVE IMAGES

Any particular corporate image or perceptions we might have is inextricably linked to a company's people—how they act, how they present themselves, and, above all, how they interact with you. As the old customer service axiom says, "Customers don't care how much you know; they care how much you care."

WHAT IT MEANS: We often think of certain companies as being friendly or being rude. Jet Blue, for example, has a reputation for being friendly and helpful, while other airlines are perceived as giving you the runaround—and not necessarily to where you want to go. Some companies micromanage the customer experience to the nth degree, leaving no contingency unscripted. Others seem to derive a strange glee from casting you into the depths of voice-mail hell, all the while intermittently reassuring you that "Your call is very important to us"—but apparently not important enough to hire a sufficient number of living, breathing customer service representatives.

ACTION PLAN: When you're on the phone or dealing with a customer in person, recognize that your entire company's reputation is on the line. The more you treat your customers with respect, empathy, and a caring, can-do attitude, the more new business you'll attract. It's as simple—and challenging—as that.

EVEN BETTER: There's a tendency in many companies to take a dim and dismissive view of customers—after all, customers can be so demanding and intrusive! They are, however, the only reason your business is still in business. Everyone in your company would do well to appreciate that and react accordingly—but you need to lead by example. Make customer service excellence an ongoing priority for your company. Hire for it. Train for it. Monitor it. Reward for it. Believe it!

KNOW THY COMPETITOR

Having competitors is not a bad thing. Their very existence proves that there is a market for your products or services. And while you may be inclined to view them as the enemy, they are also a potentially invaluable learning tool—as they can help you answer this critical question: what is it about your competitors' organizations that enable them to have any advantage over you in the marketplace?

WHAT IT MEANS: Identify and observe your competition in order to learn from their strengths and weaknesses. Observe how they run their business. Look for aspects of their business that you could adapt and those that could be improved. You can do this in all sorts of ways—by reading industry news, going to trade shows, visiting competitors' Web sites, speaking to sales reps and customers, ordering company profiles, et cetera, but never lose sight of your competition. *P.S.:* Learning from your competitors' mistakes can be amazingly cost-effective!

ACTION PLAN: Know who your top three competitors are. Identify three things that they are doing better than you are. Be honest. Now start to focus on ways your business might start to close the gap.

EVEN BETTER: When on the lookout for best practices to emulate, consider companies that are not in your exact business category. For example, banks may learn from brokerage firms or real estate companies, while retailers of books can lean from those who sell music.

RULE THIRTEEN
Turn Your
Mistakes into Tools

Because nobody is perfect, everybody makes mistakes. The best thing to do when this happens to you is to admit it, not attempt to justify it, and to learn from it. That's right—every mistake you (or even someone else) make is a learning opportunity in disguise.

WHAT IT MEANS: Naturally, you want to be perceived as a competent, can-do professional, but everybody screws up once in a while. If you don't, it probably means that your job is not challenging enough.

So when you do, try to have a mature perspective. It's not the end of the world. You will learn, grow, and move on. Don't compound your mistake by trying to paper it over or explaining it away—or looking for a scapegoat. Most of those oft-tried remedies simply won't work—and may even leave you looking worse.

ACTION PLAN: Cool off, calm down, and think it over. What exactly was your mistake? What, in hindsight, could you have done to prevent it (sometimes the answer will be "nothing"), or to minimize the consequent damage? What actions could you take to avoid such a mistake from recurring? That's your takeaway lesson—now, let it go!

EVEN BETTER: Invite manager and/or coworker feedback. Make it clear that you welcome such constructive criticism. By owning up to your mistakes and learning from them, you will not only free yourself from the impossible burden of always having to be perfect, you (and others) can grow from the experience, and you may well prevent future mistakes by nipping them in the bud.

RULE FOURTEEN
Ten Clowns Don't Make a Circus

Any business, like any circus, requires a certain amount of diversity. You need different people to fill different roles—lion tamers, trapeze artists, and human cannonballs—or the show just doesn't work.

WHAT IT MEANS: Cars have different systems and subsystems that must all do their job for the car to work—and so do companies. Other people's roles (and backgrounds, personalities, perspectives, etc.) are quite likely to vary from yours—and that's a good thing. For one thing, the characteristics that might make a great sales rep might make a terrible financial analyst (and vice versa). Second, having a diversity of thought (and thinkers) can help formulate more carefully considered decisions. Just because someone disagrees with you does not make him or her wrong. It takes all kinds to build a successful business—all kinds of skills, all kinds of positions, and all kinds of people.

ACTION PLAN: Try to be more open the next time someone at work disagrees with you. Don't take it personally. Focus on what is being said, not on who is saying it.

EVEN BETTER: Nobody in a company has a monopoly on good ideas. You can tap into the collective wisdom, creativity, and experience of your workgroup by maintaining an open pipeline for their ideas, suggestions, and feedback to proposed new projects and policies. As a wise colleague of mine often says, "If you want to think outside the box, sometimes you have to journey outside the box."

RULE FIFTEEN
PRESENTATIONS AS PERFORMANCES— TIME TO PRACTICE

To sell your ideas, products, and services in business, you need to make effective presentations—to management, to your team, to clients, and even over the phone. The challenge is that you only get one chance—so make sure you get it right.

WHAT IT MEANS: Every successful presentation requires preparation. But your preparation isn't complete until you've rehearsed your presentation thoroughly. There are reasons performers work so hard in rehearsal. It gives them greater control of their material. It builds confidence. And it gives the appearance that they're hardly working at all. The same applies to giving business presentations. Take a cue from the most experienced and accomplished public speakers and the most successful athletes, musicians, and presenters: practice, practice, practice!

ACTION PLAN: Write down your main points, put them in a logical sequence, and rehearse them out load. If possible, record yourself. This lets you fine-tune your remarks in ways that are more natural to your own speaking style. It's also more likely to point up flaws in your delivery that you can quickly correct, such as speaking too fast or too slow or without enough energy or with too much energy. If you can videotape yourself, even better!

EVEN BETTER: Go "live"—by testing your presentation before an audience. Seek out colleagues you can trust to give you honest, constructive criticism, even if it hurts. It may hurt more if you don't! Finally, don't think that by rehearsing you will rob your presentation of its vitality or somehow make your delivery seem slick or stilted. Practice actually has the opposite effect. Because it gives you greater command of your material and more confidence in yourself, you're likely to be more relaxed and able to deliver in your own natural style.

RULE SIXTEEN
LET YOUR CUSTOMERS SHOW YOU HOW TO USE YOUR PRODUCT

Your customers are telling you things every day, not necessarily by what they say, but by what they do—what they buy, what they ask, what they complain about, et cetera. Although there is value to surveys and focus group sessions, there is always some disparity between the way people think of themselves or present themselves and what they actually do. For example, people who think of themselves as healthy eaters may be consuming far more junk food than they might imagine—or would ever admit.

WHAT IT MEANS: Listening to your customers is worthwhile, but don't overlook the hard evidence of what your customers actually buy from you. Try to identify buying patterns and preferences and fine-tune your marketing and product mix accordingly. Marketing well requires having the knowledge and capability to cater more effectively to the needs and demonstrated preferences of different customer segments.

ACTION PLAN: Most companies have some kind of customer database. Take a close, hard look at yours. Does it reveal buying patterns? If not, fix it. If it does, begin to develop strategic ideas or initiatives directly driven by customer spending data.

EVEN BETTER: Develop a wish list for your ideal customer information management system and determine how much of it you can practically implement. Your customers are voting with their dollars and purchasing decisions every day—what are they telling you? By answering this question as precisely as possible, you will be able to make smarter marketing, product development, and customer service decisions—and be more on the money about your product/service offerings to various customer segments.

RULE SEVENTEEN
LOOK PEOPLE IN THE EYE

E-mail, intranets, faxes, voice mail. They're fine for accelerating the transfer of factual information. But when your communication involves any emotion at all or expresses a different opinion, a face-to-face meeting is by far your best bet, with a traditional, interactive, phone conversation a distant second choice. Even the popular term for such meetings, *face-to-face,* suggests an immediacy that no e-mail or phone call can match.

WHAT IT MEANS: As we get more efficient at communicating facts electronically, we tend to forget how much emotion we convey through body language and voice tone. For example, when a person uses words to disagree with someone else, their tone, posture, smile, and eye contact may at the very same time be saying, "I value and respect your opinion and enjoy working with you ... even though I disagree with you on this point."

On a group level, participative meetings give people a feeling that their opinion can be heard, and that it counts—a lot.

ACTION PLAN: Try to avoid meetings "on the fly" unless absolutely necessary. By notifying people as to when a meeting is scheduled and what will be on the agenda, you give them more time to prepare their presentation—and perhaps even to walk into the meeting with more accomplished or more to add.

EVEN BETTER: Have regularly scheduled meetings with your key managers or the members of your team. This can help keep everyone on the same page, build a productive and well-motivated team, and help you gain the benefit of various perspectives. Also, when praising or criticizing someone individually, try to do so in person.

RULE EIGHTEEN
K.I.S.S., SORT OF....

I'm quite sure you're familiar with the K.I.S.S. acronym—"Keep it simple, stupid."

It's gratuitously blunt perhaps, but an effective way to make the point that sometimes we just need to focus on the key points and not get lost in the details. The reality is that you cannot possibly plan for all of the contingencies that might occur. The solution: keep it simple. But not too simple.

WHAT IT MEANS: Train your employees well on the basics of their jobs. They should have a clear understanding of your goals and their responsibilities— but don't try to plan for every contingency. Rather, hire intelligent people, clue them in on what you're trying to achieve, and then make sure that they have a clear sense of what to do when "the rules" don't clearly apply.

ACTION PLAN: Delegate enough flexibility to employees so that when the unexpected occurs, they can respond in a timely and effective manner. Rather than rules develop guidelines and communicate their underlying rationale.

EVEN BETTER: To reinforce "outside of the box" decision making, make sure to recognize and praise employees who demonstrate initiative. When poor decisions have been made, don't punish—teach! What could have been considered, but was not? What, in retrospect, would have been a smarter course of action?

DON'T BECOME A SLAVE TO YOUR E-MAIL

E-mail is great. It can ease and expedite your communications, help you check the status of current projects, and even help you market yourself or your company—but there's a downside too. If you're the type of person who goes into shock every time you've been away from your e-mail for a few hours, then you know what I mean.

WHAT IT MEANS: Don't let your in-box run your day. As tempting as it may be to obsessively check your e-mail, your cyberspace inbox is not your to-do list. From a time-management and productivity perspective, you're better off setting aside a block of time for e-mail—then give yourself long uninterrupted stretches to get regular work done. If a response will take less than two minutes, do it immediately. If it takes longer, be very sure that responding quickly is really the very best use of your time.

ACTION PLAN: How often should you check your e-mail? Some people suggest only twice a day, but the correct answer really depends on exactly what your job and responsibilities are. Also, keep your replies brief and on point. Avoid the urge to elaborate or justify ad nauseum—it's not necessary, and it wastes time. Think memo, not PowerPoint presentation.

EVEN BETTER: Do you find yourself replying to the same kind of e-mail—or issuing the same kind of e-mail request—time and time again? If so, why reinvent the wheel? Create a folder of boilerplate e-mail replies—and benefit from the amazing power of "copy and paste."

Tomorrow Is Another Day

Just as a well-run business follows a budget in spending money, an effective businessperson should also follow a budget in spending time. In the real world, most things take longer than planned, and there are always unanticipated "fires," small or otherwise, to handle. Overbooking yourself isn't just impractical, it can boost your stress into the red zone.

WHAT IT MEANS: Working with a realistic schedule is much more productive than you might think. Chances are, you'll be less frazzled, tense, and rushed. Besides, who wants to begin each day feeling that the clock is already against him? Success in business is more of a marathon—not a sprint.

This is particularly important for entrepreneurs, who tend to juggle a lot of hats—and often let their focus become diverted to the crisis of the moment. That may be very dramatic, but it's just not a very good way to allocate your time. The one thing in business that you can always expect is the unexpected—so why not plan for it?

ACTION PLAN: Think of your schedule as a container into which you need to fit a limited number of objects—you'll become more selective about what you put in. If you visualize that way, you'll fill your days more efficiently.

EVEN BETTER: Leave some breathing room for relaxing and thinking, and for a buffer in case something comes up unexpectedly. Of course, there are inevitably going to be some days when your schedule runs you—but try to keep those days to an absolute minimum.

RULE TWENTY-ONE
EVERYONE IS IN SALES

A sales-centric company is a more successful company—and that begins by eliminating the all-too-prevalent "that's not my department" mentality. Whether you're in accounting, research, or any department of a company at all, your willingness to become more sales oriented can reap huge dividends—not only for your company, but for your career as well.

WHAT IT MEANS: Relax—this rule doesn't mean that you have to make sales calls on your way home from work or hand out company brochures to strangers on the street. What you do need to realize is that selling opportunities do occur outside of regular channels or office hours, and it's one of your professional responsibilities to respond to them.

If you're like most people, you probably have some resistance to selling. The stereotype of the used-car salesman, with his high-pressure tactics, is still very much with us—but that's really not what selling is. Selling is being naturally enthusiastic and positive about your company. Selling is recognizing when people's needs or interests connect to something your company offers, and making a polite introduction.

ACTION PLAN: Simply be alert to the opportunities as they present themselves—while making small talk at a social gathering ... while traveling on vacation ... or while letting people know what you do. As they say, sales is a "contact sport"—so anytime you can add to people's awareness of what your company does, you are adding a link to the chain. If you let just two new people a week know what your company does, that's 100 people a year.

EVEN BETTER: Stay current on your company's products and services as well as any other news or information that would help you to present your company in a positive and appealing way. The more you know, the more important information you'll be able to draw on when necessary.

RULE TWENTY-TWO
LET RELIABILITY BE YOUR WATCHWORD

Let's face it—it's a risky world we live in. There's cutthroat competition, human error, interpersonal friction, organizational inertia, and any number of unanticipated factors that can come along and screw up your project. That's why the business world will always value someone who's as good as his or her word—or better.

WHAT IT MEANS: Your word is your bond, so take your commitments very seriously. If you promise to do something, do it. If for some reason you can't get it done, notify whomever you promised ASAP and offer feasible alternatives. Nevertheless, reliability isn't just about being trustworthy; it's also about doing everything you can to reinforce an image and reputation for reliability. True professionals: show up on time for meetings; deliver consistently good work on budget and on time; admit when they're wrong and do their best to fix it; remain on an even keel emotionally; don't undercut authority or disparage others; can be counted upon to "sweat the details," manage their way around glitches, and get things done.

ACTION PLAN: Apply the above criteria to yourself. Is there an area or two in sore need of improvement? What, exactly, would you do differently? Also, think of three times in your career when your reliability factor took a direct hit. With the benefit of hindsight and experience, what proactive or corrective action could you have taken?

EVEN BETTER: Look for people in your organization or network who you feel are paragons of reliability—and then attempt to emulate them. Find out what makes them tick or seek their counsel on any pending reliability challenge. Also, make it clear to your reports that you expect superior reliability, and make it clear up front what that standard demands.

RULE TWENTY-THREE
ADVERTISING IS GOOD,
PUBLICITY IS BETTER

Much can be said in the debate as to which is better—advertising or public relations. An advertising executive will tell you that PR offers short-term impact whereas advertising is more strategic. A PR executive will counter that good PR will offer both strategic and immediate impact. It's become apparent though: put your money on the promotional power of publicity every time.

WHAT IT MEANS: Publicity requires a lot of effort, but it's worth it. Let's face it, the world is deluged with advertising. The average person is subjected to thousands of advertising impressions each day. Unless you have the budget for a major advertising campaign, your message is just not likely to break through all that clutter. There's also an ever-worsening credibility problem. People tend not to believe ads because they know those ads are only there to sell them something. On the other hand, when people read what they perceive as legitimate news sources, they view that information as more objective and reliable. What they (and you) may not realize is that a good amount of the non-hard news comes from press releases and publicists doing their jobs—so if you have a product or service that is newsworthy, you can often get people to know about it for free.

ACTION PLAN: Issue press releases on a regular basis. Develop a media list of local press and relevant trade periodicals. Keep in mind that journalists are looking for news, not just self-serving hype, so make their job easier—and positive results more likely—by developing interesting story angles to go with your press releases.

EVEN BETTER: Plan an event to which you invite others in your industry—and the press. Trade shows are an excellent opportunity for this. You can seize the moment by introducing a new product or making some other type of major PR splash. And it's a great way to further develop your media contacts.

RULE TWENTY-FOUR
DON'T LET YOUR
PAST HAUNT YOU

No matter how awful your previous employer was, no matter how terrible your boss was, no matter how evil your coworkers were, never, ever burn your bridges behind you. It doesn't matter how bad things were—don't take it out on your boss or coworkers in person before you leave. The "take this job and shove it" attitude will get you absolutely nothing except a temporary feeling of superiority. From a long-term perspective, such a feeling is a luxury that might be more expensive than you think. Staying on good terms with ex-bosses and coworkers—past, present, and future—is simply a smart long-term career strategy.

WHAT IT MEANS: There's always an upside to maintaining as many positive working relationships as possible. Burned bridges can and do come back to haunt you—in ways you can never predict. Whether you're leaving the company or someone in the company is leaving you, leave the door open by parting on good terms. You never know what opportunities might result further down the road.

ACTION PLAN: Write a friendly good-bye note whenever someone is leaving. A handwritten note or card is preferable, but make the effort to let the person know that he or she will be missed. Everyone knows about the importance of making a good first impression, but making a positive final impression is also worthwhile.

EVEN BETTER: Get in touch with former coworkers six months or so down the road. What have they been up to? What have you been up to? Make sure you have their new contact information (or vice versa). Periodic follow-ups like this are a good way of keeping your network active, and making the effort to stay in touch (however briefly) is usually appreciated. It's good to stay on good terms and in contact with as many people as possible.

Make Sure to Get the Whole Team on the Same Field

When you're working on a project or task that involves more than one person, it's almost always a good idea to have everyone meet, physically or over the phone, at the outset. This kickoff meeting helps ensure that everyone understands the big picture, it helps formally establish the team and bond the members, and it helps everyone at least begin on the same page. Quite often, the wisdom of a group will be more than the sum of its parts.

WHAT IT MEANS: People simply do better work when they understand how their efforts fit into a larger whole, so the motivational value of this practice alone is quite substantial, but having an introductory project meeting has other advantages too. People prefer working with people that they know or, at least, have met—and such a meeting can establish the lines of communication necessary to achieve the work ahead. Critical junctures can be identified. Deadlines can be more easily delineated, and things to do can be delegated on the spot.

Thirty minutes with everyone in the room can save days of telephone tag, e-mail reply lag, and "I'm still waiting to hear from Jim" delays, so go ahead—schedule the meeting!

ACTION PLAN: Meetings are almost impossible to pull together on very short notice—so, if at all possible, don't! Do your best to give people adequate notice as to when meetings will take place and what will be on the agenda. If certain people will be making formal presentations at a meeting, make sure that they know this and are well prepared. Being that specific about it makes it more real and more important in people's minds.

EVEN BETTER: At the end of your meeting, make it a point to schedule the next meeting. It's easier to gain this kind of group commitment when everyone is all together. People will be rushing out and saying, "I'll call you later." Nevertheless, insist on setting a firm next-meeting date right then and there.

CHANGE IS MANDATORY, GROWTH IS OPTIONAL

This might be the least original law in this entire book, but it's so important that I just couldn't take the risk of leaving it out. Greek philosopher Heraclitus noted the constancy of change in life nearly 2,500 years ago—and what was true then is just as true today. Ironically, this is probably the one business rule that has remained constant.

WHAT IT MEANS: Society operates twenty-four hours a day, every day, at a fast pace. Computer technology is outdated almost instantly. Companies make long-term plans for five years, at most. Does this mean you throw in the towel because all planning is futile? Well, no. But it does mean that you can never afford to rest too long on your laurels. Never-ending change is the only consistent, predictable thing in our lives.

Best-selling products, no matter how hot, have a finite life cycle. You can and should try to extend it—but no joyride lasts forever. Things that were cutting-edge just a few years ago have lost their gleaming shine. You can connect to the Internet? Yawn. That connection today needs to be broadband—and wireless. Most people under forty probably don't even remember carbon paper. Things change.

ACTION PLAN: It's been said that the best way to predict the future is to invent it. That's a smart strategy. If you keep a critical, proactive perspective on your career and your company, you'll be ahead of the game. What skills do you need to acquire? What technologies can help you do things better, cheaper, or faster? What opportunities do current market trends suggest? What are the three things that your company most needs **to change? And, above all, what's next?**

EVEN BETTER: Brainstorm with your team on a regular basis to identify and plan for needed changes in your business. Provide the team with an article that reports on some intriguing new technology or innovation that might be worth considering. The benefit of gaining fresh perspectives in addition to yours could be valuable.

CAREFUL WITH THE COMPANY'S MONEY—IT MAY WANT IT BACK

It's easy to treat an expense account as an open invitation to live large. Lots of people do just that—but don't be one of them. You don't have to count paper clips or eat at greasy-spoon diners—simply recognize that in your professional role, you are being entrusted with (among other things) the responsibility of acting as the company's caretaker of cash.

WHAT IT MEANS: Treat the company's money at least as carefully as you handle your own. This doesn't mean that you can't splurge once in a while for a great restaurant meal for your team, but easy does it. More often than not, you should avoid dining at the most expensive restaurants in town. Let them be other people's expense account picks, not yours. By doing so, the message you'll convey, both to your managers and your subordinates, is that you're a bit cautious and conservative—both good qualities for anyone who manages or handles other people's money.

Making people more aware of how much money the company is spending on them can be a good management communications strategy too. People tend to underestimate what they don't know—so if the company is paying for health insurance premiums or investing so many dollars per employee in training, that information is worth letting employees know. To be sure, not every employee will appreciate knowing the cost of each fringe benefit, but the numbers do offer tangible and objective proof that real money was spent—and that in itself can make a positive impression.

ACTION PLAN: Get bids or check prices from various suppliers to make sure you are getting competitive prices. If you haven't done this in a while, do it now. Shop around for good deals on airfare, office supplies, computer equipment, whatever. You don't have to be a cost analyst to be concerned about costs—and being consistently cost conscious can have a very healthy impact on your company's profitability.

EVEN BETTER: Discuss expenses with your coworkers and staff. Question anything you don't understand. You may be viewed as a bit of a killjoy or tightwad, but the bottom line is that it's not their money—and part of your job is to be prudent about all expenditures. Regularly monitoring all expenses is one clear way to send that message to one and all.

RULE TWENTY-EIGHT
TIME IS *Not* ON YOUR SIDE

I once asked the president of a huge company what it took to get to the top. "The same thing it took to get started," he replied, "a sense of urgency." The people who make things move in this world share this same sense of urgency! Maintaining a sense of urgency can be challenging, but as the motivational poster asks, "If you don't have time to do it right the first time, then how will you find the time to do it again?"

WHAT IT MEANS: The world is full of very competent people who honestly intend to do things tomorrow, or as soon as they can get around to it. Their accomplishments, however, seldom match those of less-talented people who appreciate the importance of getting started now.

As a manager, your ability to communicate this sense of urgency to the people who work for you is also likely to yield positive results. The best way to do this: show an interest in your people's projects and their jobs. Check on their progress, and be quick to help in any way you can. Plain and simple, things that you seem obviously interested in are much more likely to get done first and on time, so be interested and stay interested—from start to finish.

ACTION PLAN: Encourage others—and yourself—to make to-do lists and to prioritize them. Strive to do what's urgent and/or important first. Part of being an effective manager is doing what you have to do, not just what you want to do.

EVEN BETTER: Make it your business to get everything done by a certain time. Deadlines have a proven motivational value all their own. If you have certain projects on your to-do list that will take longer than a week or so, break them down into more manageable and doable stages—and handle them that way. Success is seldom accidental.

IF YOU CAN'T START THE TRENDS, MAKE SURE YOU KEEP AN EYE ON THEM

You can manage more effectively—and market yourself effectively—by knowing what is going on in your current industry. More than ever, knowledge is power, and today's market is as competitive as ever. Ignorance is one luxury you can't afford.

WHAT IT MEANS: As you develop a deeper industry knowledge base, you'll improve your own ability to more quickly grasp the implications of business trends. Don't merely collect and file the information however—think about it. How might the information covered be strategically useful? It's not good enough to be a knowledge collector; you've got to be a knowledge assimilator. Become someone who can respond to industry news and trends in a creative and thoughtful way and filter them through a strategic prism. Your experienced perspective will undoubtedly make you more of an "industry expert" too!

ACTION PLAN: How do you stay on top of news and trends in your profession or industry? Check out the business section of the newspaper, watch the business media, and stay current with economic trends that impact your industry. If you see an article that might be of interest to a colleague, or your boss, highlight the pertinent information, and add your own editorial spin. Also, read business books of interest and industry periodicals (many of which are now online) and attend tradeshows, industry seminars, and conferences.

EVEN BETTER: Also make it your business to keep up with what so-called indirect competitors are doing. This includes businesses that operate in markets outside your own but affect your customers in other ways. Their innovations and practices may not fully translate to your industry or company, but they can nevertheless be provocative food for thought.

RULE THIRTY
LEARN TO BE PROMOTABLE

Become an employee your company wants to retain and promote. If you don't know the answer to a question, know where to find it. Be aware of the structure of your business. Look at the organization chart and understand where you fit, where your department fits, how many people report to your manager, and so on.

WHAT IT MEANS: Outstanding people always manage to find a way to stand out. Seek the spotlight you deserve. Identify projects that might benefit from your participation and ask to be assigned to them. Keep track of your successes and make sure that management and other stakeholders are aware of them. Use your intelligence as if all results depended on you

ACTION PLAN: Reach an understanding about how much time a project should require before undertaking it. As you begin new assignments, check back with your supervisor or team leader periodically to confirm that you are on the right track. Don't miss deadlines. If it looks like you're going to have a problem, negotiate a revised schedule and get help. Be visible by overworking the first few months in a new position. You'll be perceived as a hard worker for much longer than that.

EVEN BETTER: Part of being promotable is learning how to promote yourself. Document your own achievements and share them with your manager from time to time. You don't have to wait until official performance reviews to do this—although that is always a good time to polish your presentation and portfolio of accomplishments. Also, try to gain a clear sense from your boss about how well you're doing and what you need to be doing better.

TRANSLATE NUMBERS TO ENGLISH

Learn to understand what the numbers mean—and what problems or opportunities they suggest. Companies are in business to make money—and the financial reports are the way that everyone keeps score. Without being astute in this area, you are flying blind—not a good way to travel at all.

WHAT IT MEANS: Financial reports speak their own language, and your competence in business requires that you have a basic understanding of them. Make sure you know what's in your company's financial report, how it's assembled, and how your actions affect the numbers. If you are uncertain about what these reports mean, make it your business to find out.

ACTION PLAN: Regularly review your financial performance with your boss and those reporting to you. If you see performance slipping in an area, analyze why and take action. If there's an overall performance problem but the cause is unclear, look for a financial breakdown. As you analyze the report, ask yourself, "Is there any other information that would help me?"

EVEN BETTER: You don't have to become a CPA, but there are various ways you can get up to speed. Take a class, read a book, or ask someone in finance. By and large you'll find that people really do like to teach about their specialties. Always ask for the reports you need to manage your business better, and ask for help with anything you don't understand.

RULE THIRTY-TWO
There is No Such Thing as a Secret

Keeping information confidential is one of your many professional responsibilities.

If you need to know why you can't make exceptions to disclosing secrets, just look in the mirror. Admit it—you yourself know how hard it is to keep secrets, so you have more than an inkling of how difficult it is for others to do so.

WHAT IT MEANS: In your career, you will inevitably be entrusted with confidential information—sales figures, marketing plans, trade secrets, et cetera. You will certainly be tempted to reveal this information. After all, there's a definite ego buzz to telling secrets. It shows that you're in the know. You may even tell yourself that it's OK, if the person you're talking to is not connected to your industry in any way. After all, what good is a secret if you can't tell anybody? Don't fall into that trap. There was a popular saying during World War II: "Loose lips sink ships." Well, they also compromise companies. As a manager or employee, you are also effectively a trustee of much information that was intended to go no further than you. Make sure to keep it that way.

ACTION PLAN: Write down what you know that is confidential, and keep it in a secure file. Review this file regularly, and commit yourself to ensuring that what's in there goes no further. This exercise will keep you focused on what you should not be discussing freely.

EVEN BETTER: Make sure your staff and coworkers know that you're a real hard-liner when it come to confidentiality. This is not an area to be lenient in. Be very clear as to the parameters of confidentiality regarding any company information—who can be told and who can't? Don't assume that everyone understands this concept as well as you do.

RULE THIRTY-THREE
WORK SMARTER, NOT HARDER

Working long hours is accepted by many as the essential ingredient for productivity and success. But the fact is, that assumption is quite often wrong. Sure, ninety-hour workweeks make you look busy—and they may even be the norm in your office—but if it's taking you ninety hours to do what could just as effectively be done in forty or fifty ... well, how smart is that?

WHAT IT MEANS: Success is really about how effective you are, not how long you work. The main thing to keep in mind is that quantity does not equate with quality or achievement. Burning the midnight oil may be what's expected of you. It may even be standard operating procedure—but that's exactly my point. If everyone else is doing it, then you're really doing no better than anyone else. If you truly want to be outstanding, you need to get more of the right things done.

ACTION PLAN: What does it mean to work smart? It means being aware of what you're trying to accomplish, having a clear and commanding sense of your priorities, delegating when possible, taking advantage of technology to be more productive when possible, staying organized, avoiding wasted effort, and being more focused and frugal about your time.

EVEN BETTER: Regularly evaluate what you've accomplished over the past week or two. Does it sync more or less with what you set out to accomplish? What got in the way—and was it the best use of your time? Are you delegating as much as you could? Are you micromanaging or letting things get too lax? Focus on establishing what needs to get done and getting it done, and not just on putting in long hours.

RULE THIRTY-FOUR
GET OUT OF TOWN.

If you run a local shop in town, and almost all of your customers are local, this rule does not apply to you. In today's global economy, however, some of your best customers may be outside your area. It's a good idea to visit them on occasion—you'll return with new insights, a better understanding of your customers' needs, and a reinforced customer relationship.

WHAT IT MEANS: Whether on a customer sales call or at a trade show or at a professional development seminar, leaving the confines of your office and getting out of town can be a great way to freshen your perspective, recharge your batteries, and spark some new ideas. To be sure, it's not as refreshing or relaxing as a vacation—but it's not business as usual either. Freed from the minutiae and interruptions of your daily grind, you may have the advantages of unstructured time and solitude to do some "big picture" thinking—or to learn about potentially beneficial new products, services, and skills.

ACTION PLAN: Schedule "field trips" several times each year to meet with key customers. Attend a trade show (or two) that's most relevant to your industry. Roam the aisles of exhibitors to see what's new. Attend some of the sessions or seminars. Invite some A-list customers or colleagues to lunch or dinner.

EVEN BETTER: Make notes, take pictures, and gather or request information—all to make sure that your new discoveries and planned follow-up activities don't get lost in transit. Carry a mini digital recorder to take voice notes on the fly. Also, request that new product/vendor information of particular interest be sent to your office following the show—so be sure to bring lots of business cards!

A Paper Trail Will Help You Find Your Way Back

If you've ever heard of the acronym CYA, then you know one good reason for this rule. Keeping meticulous records about who did what when isn't just critical information to have on hand if and when you are ever called on the carpet to explain or defend yourself. It also gives you the insurance of being able to recollect past actions and decisions without having to exclusively rely on your memory.

WHAT IT MEANS: What happened at the last meeting or in your project update discussion last night might be fresh in your mind this morning, but it won't be three months or three years from now. If there is no written record, there is no evidence, and it becomes a matter—often an impossible-to-prove matter—of "he said, she said." Everything you do, say, or agree to in business is on the record in a certain sense. By documenting as much as possible, you are effectively ensuring that this record stays clear and secure.

ACTION PLAN: Get into the habit of taking notes of what happens—during meetings, phone calls, and even less formal situations. Learning how to use a PC-based notes or PDA program is worth the effort, as it makes your notes retrievable by date, names, project name, or keywords.

EVEN BETTER: Review these notes on a regular basis. They can help you prepare for meetings, future customer calls, future projects, and performance reviews (yours and your reports'). As a rule of thumb, if anything is said, done, or decided upon that you consider significant, it's worth writing down. E-mails that are relevant to this rule can easily be copied and pasted into whatever notes or contact management system you prefer.

RULE THIRTY-SIX
CREATE GOALS WORTH REACHING

Most businesspeople know that they need targets to reach for. Monthly, quarterly, and yearly sales or production quotas, both individually and organizationally, are common, but sometimes these goals don't take into account the changing nature of the market or the possibility of entering previously untapped markets.

WHAT IT MEANS: Aiming for marginal increments of what your company has always done (a 10% increase in sales) is a good start, but why not set the bar even higher? By factoring in new products, new markets, and even new ways of doing business, you can establish goals that are more bold, more out of the box—and perhaps more likely to propel your business to a whole new level. To a certain extent, organizations need to continually reinvent themselves—and goals (which have been termed "dreams with deadlines") can help motivate them to achieve this.

ACTION PLAN: Regularly review the metrics that you and your company use to gauge performance. Are they accurately reflecting the things your company needs to do? If not, consider new measuring tools and techniques. More often than not, what gets measured gets done.

EVEN BETTER: Identify three or four brand-new goals that would help your company explore new products, services, markets, and/or processes. This will undoubtedly be more challenging than factoring in a 15 percent or 20 percent increase to last year's sales—but it will also almost certainly be more worthwhile.

RULE THIRTY-SEVEN
PAMPER YOUR CUSTOMERS

Why do you suppose all evidence proves that it costs at least five times as much to sell to a new customer as to an existing customer? That's easy. Because the price is high to find a new customer, while finding an existing customer is free. It's far less expensive to retain customers—by delighting and pampering them—than it is to acquire new ones, yet most companies blatantly continue to ignore this clear and compelling rule.

WHAT IT MEANS: Pamper your existing customers. It will set you apart from 95 percent of your competition. It will help you compete on a basis other than price. It will generate repeat business. And, as word of mouth is well known to be the most effective form of advertising, it will generate a steady stream of new customers through glowing referrals. In his book *Guerilla Marketing Weapons: 100 Affordable Marketing Methods for Maximizing Profits from Your Small Business,* marketing guru Jay Conrad Levinson says, "There are few if any other marketing weapons with the power, cost-effectiveness, and economy of satisfied customers."

ACTION PLAN: Customer pampering is anything you can do that can make your customers feel recognized, appreciated, and special. It's going the extra mile. It's adding a little bit (or even more than a little bit) of "Wow" to the way you do business—coffee service in the reception area ... dropping off papers or delivering an order in person so the customer doesn't have to pick it up ... or writing a note or e-mail just to say "thanks for being our customer."

EVEN BETTER: Develop loyalty programs designed to increase overall satisfaction, encourage repeat business, and delight your best customers. You can focus on rewarding customers who have repeat purchases, such as discounts for frequent purchases, special "loyal customer only" sales, or gifts to frequent buyers. However, it is important to realize that not all freebies will work with all customers—a free T-shirt may work for one business but be perceived as "too tacky" by customers of another business—so consider this matter carefully. Surveys, focus groups, and direct discussions with customers can be helpful in this area.

RULE THIRTY-EIGHT
ALWAYS KNOW WHO'S WHO

How many times have we heard, "It's not what you know, it's who you know?" Well, it happens to be true. Your ability to transact business is based partially upon what you can do—but it is also based upon what people whom you can get to quickly can do. When it comes to getting a foot in the door or to getting "below the radar" job leads—or simply to helping customers, prospects, and other business associates out with a good referral—nothing beats your personal and professional contact list.

WHAT IT MEANS: Contacts create opportunities, so make your contact list as large and valuable as possible by regularly adding to it and being aware of possible synergies. Recent surveys state that over 60 percent of all jobs are found through networking—but whether you're looking for a new job, a new client, or a new promotion, it's key not only to establish new contacts, but to cultivate them—and that means knowing more about your contacts than just what they can do for you. Sales guru and best-selling author Harvey MacKay is well known for meticulously capturing all sorts of biographical data on his contacts—family information, birthdays, special interests, favorite sports, et cetera.

ACTION PLAN: Devote time and effort to extending your contact list and recording it in some systematic and easy-to-access manner. Many PC-based contact programs are available, or you can do it the old-fashioned Rolodex way—but do it. Some potential contact sources: industry providers, coworkers, service providers, family members, professional organizations, volunteer organizations, trade groups, sports teams (including your kids'), and alumni. Also, being more upbeat, outgoing, and genuinely interested in other people are all critical social network–building skills; working to develop them will be to your advantage.

EVEN BETTER: Revisit your contact database from time to time to refresh your awareness of specific contacts. Doing so is likely to spark a good reason for calling a few of them, and that's a good thing. A simple phone call or e-mail can open up all sorts of opportunities. After all, that's why they're called contacts.

HIRE PEOPLE MORE TALENTED THAN YOU

What is the best way to deal with problem performers? Don't hire them in the first place! Both poor and superb workers were probably already that way when you chose them, so why not make the smart choice in the first place? Believe me, it's well worth the effort!

WHAT IT MEANS: Finding and firing outstanding employees is one of the most important things a business owner or manager can do. Employees help set the tone, do the work, and deal with customers, and they're the ones on the front line. If they blow it, your business will suffer. Conversely, if you hire someone who's bright, ambitious, reliable, and self-starting, that not only makes your job easier, it frees you up to focus more on leading and growing your business. The hiring process involves three stages: preparation, searching for qualified applicants, and interviewing.

ACTION PLAN: As much as you evaluate the background, education, skills, and intelligence of a job candidate, you must also consider personality and compatibility. After all, you and your employees will be spending much time together. "Chemistry" is sometimes hard to articulate, but it's critical to consider. Make a list of the twenty most important qualities you need in the next person to fill the job, so you have a clear and comprehensive idea of what you're looking for.

EVEN BETTER: Many people rush through interviews because they're too busy or uncomfortable with the process. Don't be one of them. Develop your interview skills by reading some guides or taking a course. Take the time to prepare—and the time to form a meaningful impression of the most impressive candidates. Write down your questions beforehand, and make sure to take notes—it may be the only way you will remember the difference between Candidate A and Candidate G. Also, don't tolerate mediocrity! If you happen to make a poor hiring decision (and you will), cut your losses short by letting the person go ASAP. There can be a learning curve and some "positive intervention," but if you're not reasonably impressed with your new hire's performance, he or she is probably doing more harm than good.

ACCEPT THE RESPONSIBILITY, REGARDLESS OF THE OUTCOME

President Harry Truman had a famous sign on his desk, which read, "The buck stops here." Well, every manager would do well to develop the same attitude. Mistakes happen because people (and processes) are imperfect—and even though the error may not be your direct fault, if it happened on your watch, accept responsibility.

Nothing is more demoralizing or toxic to an organization than managers who seek to hog all the credit and divert all the blame. Honestly, how would you feel working for such a manager? Enough said!

WHAT IT MEANS: Leadership may not be as complicated as we make it. The bottom line is pretty simple: conduct yourself the way you'd want those under you to. Share the credit with everyone who helped you, and even if you actually did the lion's share of a particular task, don't trumpet that fact. Most important of all, admit your mistakes; never blame others.

ACTION PLAN: Review the last mistake you made that you were called on the carpet for. Did you accept full responsibility or did you attempt to dodge and finger-point? Would you have handled it in a different way now, in light of this rule? Many people have a very hard time ever admitting that they're wrong. As objectively as possible, ask yourself if you are one of them.

EVEN BETTER: Accept that mistakes will happen, and—leading by example—show that the emphasis should not be on blame and punishment, but rather on learning. Who did what is less important than considering what might be done to keep the mistake from happening again. Also, don't kick a good employee when she is down. People feel bad enough when they screw up. It might be very motivating and "remoralizing" to take that person aside and recommend that she not get too worked up over the error. She is still a valued member of your team. It's a lesson—perhaps a painful and/or expensive lesson— but it was, after all, a mistake. You will both learn from it, and you will move on.

MAKE SURE YOU ARE SEEN

Businesses spend significant money on advertising campaigns and marketing programs to get themselves noticed—otherwise they get lost in the ever-competitive marketplace.

On the individual level, you have to "advertise" yourself too—not with slick brochures (unless you're a self-employed professional)—but by the various ways you can make a positive and memorable impression as you do your job.

WHAT IT MEANS: Simply showing up and being a quiet, dependable "cog" no longer cuts it. Of course, shameless and shrill self-promotion doesn't cut it either—and could soon give you a reputation as being spectacularly obnoxious. There is another way. You need to get people to know you and to value your contributions. You need to be known for your reliability and bright ideas. You need to let your manager know that you're ready for more. Most of all, you need to develop a track record of performance and achievements so stellar that they practically glow and speak for themselves.

ACTION PLAN: Make yourself more visible by sharing ideas in meetings, writing an article for the company newsletter (or a trade magazine), and volunteering for new projects—especially those most likely to showcase your skills or bring you in contact with other departments. Keep a list of all your achievements (a must for performance reviews). Let your boss know that you are eager to take any seminar that could enhance your professional skills. If you've attended a seminar, offer to give colleagues and/or team members a quick summary.

EVEN BETTER: Take your own unofficial agenda to meetings. In other words, be prepared to advance your ideas (or rebut others') by being fluent on their key selling points and being able to present whatever supporting evidence you can. The idea is to participate and meaningfully contribute, not to dominate. That alone is likely to get you noticed—but so will the quality of your work, your extended relationships with people throughout the organization, and your positive commitment to making a difference. Real go-getters inevitably achieve more—so get out there and get noticed!

DOUBLE-CHECK THE BOOKS

Every business gets bills—lots of them. All too often, these bills are not carefully scrutinized; they're approved far too easily. As long as a bill relates back to a valid purchase order, a check will be issued. But the fact is, more systematic scrutiny can detect and even help avert overcharges, whether intentional or not.

WHAT IT MEANS: Don't accept every bill at face value. Just because it looks official and is neatly computer-printed does not make it accurate. In particular, bills from professionals (advertising agencies, law firms, computer consultants) can be inflated, especially if you never question exactly what services and billing rate they reflect. You don't want to haggle over every bill, but it's a good cost-control measure to question whatever you don't understand and to demand a clear and detailed accounting. Also, you may be able to negotiate a slight discount for prompt payment—and it costs nothing for you to ask.

ACTION PLAN: Make sure that every bill crosses your desk. Keep a file open for reviewing bills regularly, once every week or two. Be very clear what you're paying for. Is it in line with previous charges? If not, why not? If there's a question or concern, don't hesitate to contact the vendor or service provider. There's no need to be nasty or accusatory about it—and there is definite proactive value to sending the signal that you don't just rubber-stamp every invoice that crosses your desk.

EVEN BETTER: Shop around from time to time to get competitive bids, and make sure your coworkers and employees do the same. Let your vendors and service suppliers know when you're not happy with a price increase. Make it consistently clear that you will not hesitate to take your business elsewhere if you're not getting truly competitive pricing.

RULE FORTY-THREE
BREAK BAD BUSINESS HABITS

As a conscientious and determined businessperson, you do everything in your power to make smart decisions and take fruitful actions. Sure, you do your best to avoid mistakes, but you may still be making bad moves every day. They're not the kind of errors that will stand out to you, because you're used to making them. They're bad business habits—knee-jerk, routine actions made without forethought but carrying plenty of consequences. And because they come to you so naturally, you may find nothing wrong with them.

WHAT IT MEANS: In business, as in life, there are all kinds of habits that get in the way of working with others, being more productive, and doing your best. Maybe you send too many e-mails or check them too often. Maybe you waste a good half hour or more every morning drinking coffee or making small talk or just fiddling around in general before settling down to work. Perhaps you're too abrasive, too loud, or given to interrupting other people. Maybe you've mistaken "business casual" for "sloppy." Nobody's perfect, and everyone has weaknesses—but if your bad business habits are getting in the way of your effectiveness and reputation, it's your job to start working on them. Don't wait until someone has to bring them to your attention. By then, it may already be too late.

ACTION PLAN: Bad business habits, like all habits, are hard to break. It's an automated action triggered over and over. Once you recognize your habit is hurtful, you're halfway there. Now try to catch yourself in the act and stop it in its tracks. Then tell yourself what you should do instead. With persistence, you can reprogram yourself.

EVEN BETTER: Work with a business coach to identify and improve your weaknesses. His or her objectivity and expertise in these matters are two solid advantages that you just can't bring to the table by yourself. To locate a good coach, ask some of your contacts (outside your company—you want to keep this confidential), do a Web search, or look for ads in your local business papers. They are not too hard to find.

RULE FORTY-FOUR
Use Common Sense

Sometimes you can get so caught up in the inner details of your business or so dazzled by the initial glow of a promising idea that your judgment takes a time-out, if not a leave of absence. When that happens, you don't need rosy spreadsheet projections or masterpiece PowerPoint presentations or even a Harvard M.B.A. You need a reality check—also known as common sense.

WHAT IT MEANS: Common sense in business is more than knowledge, facts, and figures. It is making reasonable assumptions, having reality-based expectations, and considering alternative possibilities when things don't go as smoothly as you planned. Common sense tells you that just because you badly want an idea or new product to be a huge success doesn't mean that it will happen. You have to do your homework. You have to think things through. In the real world, there can be many bumps, pitfalls, and detours on the way to success. Your job as a manager is to anticipate and deal with them as reasonably and comprehensively as possible—and not be seduced by the razzle-dazzle of hype or the boss's pet idea.

ACTION PLAN: Getting emotionally attached to the successful outcomes of your projects is understandable, and that's not a bad thing. Visions of success can be a great motivator for you to do your best to realize your goals. But you need yardsticks and research in place to objectively measure progress and possibilities. You may anticipate market needs, but you can't force them. Be ready to jettison pet projects and campaigns that are not measuring up despite repeated strategic interventions. It's the commonsense move.

EVEN BETTER: To avoid being blindsided by your own subjectivity, make sure you get clear and honest feedback from others on your team. That's why it's so important to create a business environment in which your senior management team can disagree with you. Gaining the benefit of group feedback is a good way to reality-check new strategies and plans. Also, invest in some well-designed market research. In business, facts always trump opinions or expectations—and an ounce of on-target market research is much more sensible than a ton of expensive (and avoidable!) failure.

THE BEST WAY TO FIND SOMETHING IS TO ACTUALLY LOOK FOR IT

Sometimes the phone number is in the white pages—and sometimes you may have to call twelve people and search the Internet for hours to track down the information you need. The more you can think out of the box to get information and solve problems, the more successful you're likely to be.

WHAT IT MEANS: Many of us have been spoiled by Google and the near-instant access to information enabled by the Internet. Be that as it may, there are times when you'll need to look elsewhere and/or dig a bit deeper. Resourcefulness and persistence are two qualities that work well together and will give you a clear and considerable advantage in every business. You'll read it in almost every other classified ad—companies are looking for people who have what it takes to solve problems. That might involve creativity, but it also requires more—a can-do attitude, a willingness to own the problem, and the persistence to make those twelve calls if that's what it takes.

ACTION PLAN: Like the highway sign says, consider alternate routes. The easiest way to get something done may not always work—so be willing to pursue various possibilities. Also, don't be the kind of employee who brings only problems to your boss. Make sure that they are accompanied by recommended solutions.

EVEN BETTER: Ask for help. Your "first tier" should probably be people who you believe might have experience relevant to the problem you're trying to solve. For example, you might ask a marketing director at another company to recommend a good freelance graphics designer or copywriter—but don't limit your search to the usual suspects. People know people who know yet other people—so putting the word out there could yield more valuable feedback than you might suspect.

RULE FORTY-SIX
SAVE, SAVE, SAVE

Everyone knows that you're supposed to back up your data files (if not your complete system)—but many people don't get into the habit of doing it until it's too late. You can save yourself a ton of pain by taking a more proactive approach.

WHAT IT MEANS: Backing up your data should be at the top of your computer maintenance list, right next to virus protection. Without data backup or virus protection, you are running the risk of losing your data. And it will happen—it's only a matter of when. To quote a tech-savvy friend of mine, "There are only two types of hard drives—the ones that have failed and the ones that will fail." Yes, normally hard drives will live for years without incident. But eventually they will die. It might happen gradually, by more and more bad clusters accumulating until most of the drive is unusable. Or it might happen suddenly—like a bolt of lightning that fries your hard drive.

ACTION PLAN: The first step in having a backup plan is to decide what data to back up. All of your documents? Your e-mails? Your contacts database? Your bookmarks or list of favorite Web sites? You probably won't want to lose any of this information—so don't! Backing up means keeping a copy of your important files in a separate location for retrieval in case of an emergency. Keeping a copy of them in another folder on the same hard drive though is not a good idea. Put it on a separate medium. Preferably, you have two backups on two separate types of media in two places. Typical data-storage choices are CDs, external hard drives, and the relatively new USB mini flash drives that can be attached to your key chain (although their storage capacity is more limited).

EVEN BETTER: The backup concept isn't just for computers. Just as you might have alternate routes in mind for getting to work, strive to have contingency plans in place when equipment or systems fail. If your copier broke down today and you urgently needed to make copies of something, what would you do?

PERCEPTION IS REALITY

Books are judged by their covers, houses are appraised by their curb appeal, and people are initially evaluated on how they choose to dress and behave. In a perfect world, this is not fair, moral, or just. What's inside should count a great deal more. And eventually it usually does, but not right away. In the meantime, a lot of opportunities can be lost.

WHAT IT MEANS: Thirty seconds—social psychologists studying the impact of image have determined that's how long it takes for someone meeting you to form a whole laundry list of impressions about your character and abilities. In those thirty seconds, people will form those impressions based almost entirely on what they see—your clothes, hairstyle, carriage, smile, and the rest of your nonverbal communications. The takeaway lesson: appearances *do* count.

ACTION PLAN: Most people are quite attuned to dressing for success when it comes to job interviews, but the concept should extend beyond there. If you're presenting at a meeting or meeting with a key customer, step it up a notch. Give some thought to your business wardrobe, and be prepared to dress appropriately for several business environments. Guys: ask your wife, girlfriend, or a fashion-literate friend for help if you need to. Remember, business casual is not the same as sloppy. Keep in mind that the suit-and-tie look is not always the way to go. In the business world, it's more a matter of "When in Rome … "—so do some advance scouting to find out how the natives dress.

EVEN BETTER: Package appeal isn't just for how you look and dress—it's about how your work looks too. E-mails and reports riddled with typos look just as sloppy as a tie with a big grease stain. Reports that are more professionally formatted—and packaged—are likely to be viewed more seriously. If you don't know the various Word formatting tricks and report cover options that can give your work a spiffy look, either delegate the task to someone who does or learn them. By paying some attention to how we package ourselves and our work, we can create a more professional, more positive, and more likely-to-succeed impression.

DEVELOP A COMPELLING ELEVATOR SPEECH

You're in an elevator and in walks the prospect you've been trying to reach for a year. You've got fifteen seconds to make an impression. What do you say?

"Hi, my name is Austin Frye, I'm in real estate."

Or...

"Hi, I'm Arnie Belder, the freelance writer who's been leaving you all those messages." or

"Hi, my name is Elaine Teller, and I'm an executive recruiter."

Blah! Bland! Boring! And what's even worse, you have blown a major, albeit time-limited, opportunity to create a more sparkling first impression. You need an elevator speech—your own personally delivered ad that you never have to pay for. Quite the contrary, it will pay for you!

WHAT IT MEANS: In the time it takes to ride an elevator with a stranger (about fifteen seconds), you have the opportunity to not only make a great first impression, but to demonstrate your professionalism, position yourself, network, and begin to extend your sphere of influence. Are you making the most of your fifteen seconds of fame? An elevator speech is a great opening positioning message that's engaging, memorable, and a great conversation starter. Every businessperson and professional should have one.

ACTION PLAN: Develop your own elevator speech and practice it until it becomes as natural an extension of yourself as your right hand. Don't forget to maintain eye contact and to smile. Whether you open with a provocative statement, a bit of mystery, or something funny, the objective is to grab a stranger's attention. Starting out by simply stating, "I'm a financial planner" is just too vanilla. Your challenge is to cast your occupation in its most ennobling light, to captivate your listener. For example, a nutritionist teaches people "how to behave in front of food," and there's an imaginative IRS agent who tells people he's a government fund-raiser. What is it that you do in your occupation that would be mostly likely to interest a stranger?

EVEN BETTER: Get feedback on your elevator speech from colleagues and friends. Many elevator speeches end with a question to both involve the listener and glean new information that helps qualify the listener in the speaker's eyes.

A caterer might ask questions about the nature and frequency of special events requiring catering services, or who the company contact is for such services. Questions that can't be answered with just a yes or no will elicit meaningful information to help the speaker determine whether a good fit exists.

KEEP YOUR INTEGRITY

In an ideal world, making compromises or unclear moral choices would not be an issue. People would always do the right thing—and so would you. The world we live in is obviously quite different. There is more than a touch of gray, morally, to many business dealings, and there are more than a few people who fit the term *ethically challenged*. You may not be able to change them or the world, but you might have to work with them.

WHAT IT MEANS: Espousing perfect behavior 24/7 is not realistic, and it's not what this rule is about. It's more about keeping your actions aligned with your values, about bending here and there without breaking, and about having a clear and conscious sense of where to draw the line between acceptable and unacceptable behavior. Integrity is the foundation of character and the cornerstone of your reputation in business. Once it's broken, it may be exceedingly difficult to fix. Most of all, it's about honesty—being honest with yourself, honest enough to admit when something just doesn't feel right, and honest enough to realize that cutting corners morally can rapidly become a very slippery slope.

ACTION PLAN: Ask yourself this question: what are your most important values in life? Your answer will reveal an enormous amount about you. What would you pay for, sacrifice for, suffer for, and fight for? What would you stand up for, or refuse to lie down for? What are the values that you hold most dear? Think these questions through carefully, and when you get a chance, write down your answers.

EVEN BETTER: If you have some reservations about doing something, sleep on it. Whatever qualms you might have about a certain morally dubious business activity could be your conscience sending you a red alert. In study after study, the quality of integrity, or a person's adherence to values, ranks as the number one quality sought in every field. When it comes to determining whom they will do business with, customers rank the honesty of a salesperson as the most important single quality. And even if that weren't true, maintaining your integrity will help you sleep better at night and be more comfortable with who you are during the day.

RULE FIFTY
LISTEN TO WHAT OTHER PEOPLE ARE SAYING

Sometimes you might be so convinced of the value of a particular idea or decision that you really don't want anyone else's opinion or good judgment—or even the facts—to get in the way. That's exactly when adhering to this rule can prevent you from making a hasty, ill-conceived, and usually expensive mistake.

WHAT IT MEANS: It is one thing to have the courage of your convictions, but it is quite another to tune out what may be some very worthwhile feedback. You may be at a meeting and apparently engaged in soliciting feedback, and you may even feign interest, but if you have already decided to cling to your opinion no matter what, then your actions are superficial and not very useful. You need to remain open to the possibility that your colleagues' and coworkers' opinions really are worth considering, even if you do not ultimately heed them.

ACTION PLAN: Sharpen your listening skills by sticking to the basics. Make eye contact. Focus on what's being said—taking notes can keep your attention at attention. Recap what's being said to make sure you understand it. Ask open-ended questions (questions that can't be answered with a simple yes or no) to draw out what others are really thinking. Also, be sensitive to the feelings behind the message. People tend to be wary of openly disagreeing with their manager, so they may be quite hesitant to do so. It's up to you to create the atmosphere and send the signals that say it's OK to disagree.

EVEN BETTER: Following the discussion, circulate a memo to summarize the various viewpoints presented. Ask for further clarification if necessary. Invite people to further comment on your summary—or to add any points you might have missed. This can ensure that you gain the benefit of everyone's feedback.

RULE FIFTY-ONE
DON'T NEGLECT YOUR HEALTH

It's been said that in business, only the most fit survive. Believe it! If you're not in solid shape physically, it's a lot harder to be in peak shape mentally or emotionally. You'll get fatigued more easily. Stress will frazzle you more. You may get moody, depressed, or short-tempered. Plain and simple, that's not you at your best—but being at your best is where you have to be to succeed.

WHAT IT MEANS: Your body is your business—your most personal business—so it's worth taking good care of it. Exercise regularly. Adopt healthier eating habits. Quit smoking, and watch your alcohol intake. Get the rest you need. And pace yourself. The principles of healthy living do not get checked at the door when you get to work. Indeed, they apply as much there as anywhere. The more fit you are, the more energy you'll have and the brighter your mood is likely to be. Fatigue can affect the quality of your thinking and the quality of your work. If you find yourself conking out in the middle of the afternoon, your body is trying to tell you something. Listen to it.

ACTION PLAN: Make a healthy living plan for yourself. Don't try to reinvent your lifestyle overnight—that's an almost certain setup for failure—but try to change your habits gradually. Perhaps you could limit your fast-food meals to two or three a week. Maybe you could take a walk during lunch or every evening (doing the latter can help you sleep), cut back on the drinking, and give yourself the benefit of an extra hour or two of sleep. Joining a gym, taking a yoga class, getting more active, eating more fruits and vegetables? All good stuff. Just pick a few new healthy habits to start, and start them!

EVEN BETTER: Be aware of hereditary health problems in your family and be especially attuned to them. Also, make the effort to become more health-literate. There is no shortage of books, magazines, and Web sites that can give you plenty of practical tips on how to start living healthier. And, like the commercial says, you're worth it!

RULE FIFTY-TWO
LEARN B&E: BREAKING AND ENTERING NEW MARKETS

New customers are the lifeblood of any business, but markets are finite, and complete market penetration is simply unrealistic. So how is a business to grow? By exploring new geographic and demographic markets—and perhaps, by retooling your existing products and services to better fit the needs of these new markets.

WHAT IT MEANS: Too many business owners limit themselves by accepting the status quo in terms of where their offerings could be sold. We really do live in a global economy, so why not take advantage of it? If your product has been successful locally, why not consider distributing it more widely? If your sales are limited to the United States, why not explore the possibility of exporting? If your attempts at online selling or catalog placement have been less than spectacular, maybe you're just not doing it right. All of these avenues, not to mention other industries or population segments you just haven't thought of yet, represent significant opportunities to take your business to the next level.

ACTION PLAN: Do your homework. Many of these "brave new markets" require special knowledge and expertise to enter. If you or no one on staff has that experience, you should consider hiring a consultant or firm that can help make it happen. Needless to say, no foray into a new market should be hasty or halfhearted. Develop a plan. Allocate some dollars. Try to form strategic partnerships. Whatever you do, treat these plans with the utmost of importance. They might not only affect the future of your business, they might ensure the future of your business.

EVEN BETTER: Do focus-group market research to determine how new market segments might respond to your current product/service line. What products/services are most likely to succeed? What modifications might be of greatest value? Finally, keep in mind that it is no failure to fall short of realizing all that we might dream. The failure is to fall short of dreaming all that we might realize.

RULE FIFTY-THREE
TREAT YOUR A-LIST LIKE STARS

A business that goes the extra mile earns the respect, loyalty, and referrals of its customers. We've already established the primary importance of treating all of your customers well. Great service makes great business sense. That said, some of your customers—perhaps 10 to 20 percent of them—are your best customers. And it's smart business to do what you can to treat them even better.

WHAT IT MEANS: Your relationship with your best customers could appropriately be viewed as a courtship. You want to show how much you love them in the hope that they will continue to love you right back. This is not so much a science as an art—the art of creating extraordinary impressions. What can you do to cultivate "Wow" and delight? Something that makes them exclaim, "Wow, no other business has ever done that for me!" It's a challenge to be sure—but if you solve it, you've gained one of the most precious assets any business can have: a lifelong, loyal, and 100 percent delighted customer (and perhaps even a few more through word-of-mouth referrals).

ACTION PLAN: First, establish the criterion for determining who your best customers are. Is it frequency of purchase or purchase volume or some combination thereof? Then, do what you can to get closer. If you're a storeowner, greet them by name when they visit your store. Find out what they like, so you can alert them to new items or special sales that may be of interest. Then, brainstorm a variety of ways in which you can go the extra mile for them. Perhaps a special customer appreciation/sales event for VIP customers only. The rule of thumb is to carefully consider what your best customers expect—and then do what you can to exceed it.

EVEN BETTER: Not everything you do for a top customer should be sales related. People appreciate being appreciated even when they don't buy something—and this is one relationship that you want to be as long-term as possible. Also, mix it up. Even the most delightful surprise—leaving a gift fruit basket or a mint on the pillow—becomes tired and trite after it's been done a few times. There should never be anything routine about wowing your best customers.

Know Your Strengths

Most people build their career mainly on their qualifications and experience. Unfortunately, they ignore the most important asset they have for achieving success: their own strengths. Unless we know our strengths and use them, we risk getting into occupations that do not suit us—or performing well below our potential in whatever endeavor we choose.

WHAT IT MEANS: If you can accept the fact that you're not perfect, it reasonably follows that you have certain strengths—skills, characteristics, talents—and weaknesses. By knowing what they are, you can leverage your strengths to your best advantage while proactively managing your weaknesses (by being more prepared, by assigning certain responsibilities and tasks to others, etc.) so that you are more effective in whatever you do. By not allowing yourself to be sabotaged by your own shortcomings, you can become much better at getting out of your own way—and that's a definite strength!

ACTION PLAN: Discover your own strengths and weaknesses. What are your five top qualities? Are you good at writing or presenting? Staying organized? Managing others? Teaching? Analyzing trends? Being persistent? To make this list as accurate as possible, try to link your strengths and weaknesses to past experiences. You may start to notice patterns and trends that were not previously apparent. Finally, seek feedback from others. Most strengths and weaknesses have a way of advertising themselves.

EVEN BETTER: Once you have a keener understanding of what you're good at, try to take on those projects (and even those jobs) that will showcase those positives more often. For example, if you're a good speaker, maybe you should be doing that more, either internally or before customers. Conversely, if being disorganized has been a perennial detour to your professional progress, learn what it takes to become more organized—or entrust that task to an assistant. Generally, teams function more effectively when each member has more of an opportunity to exercise his or her strengths.

RULE FIFTY-FIVE
LEAVE EMOTION AT THE DOOR

We've all heard the horror stories about the "boss from hell." Perhaps you've had the misfortune of suffering under one of these emotionally incontinent jerks yourself. The yelling. The blowups over relatively minor matters. The dubious ability of being able to reduce subordinates to tears. If you've seen such workplace brutality or been victimized by it, then you already know: there must be a better way.

WHAT IT MEANS: We all have emotional swings—periods when we are full of optimism and life seems great, nothing can go wrong. And then there are those other times, when we think life stinks. When we're depressed or negative, we may be tempted to inflict our worst moments on others. After all, misery does love company. Nevertheless—and this is critical—such emotional splattering is not good for business. It can cause you to make the wrong decision and take the wrong action. It can tank morale. And it can erode respect for and belief in your leadership abilities.

ACTION PLAN: Manage your emotional swings to avoid pitfalls that lead to stress. Accept defeats and disappointments without letting them ruin your whole day. Tell yourself that no other person or situation "makes" you angry. You make yourself angry. Enter potentially anger-arousing situations on yellow alert. Let your shield be the knowledge that your wrath is ultimately unproductive and unbecoming. If you want to be perceived as the consummate professional, then be the consummate professional.

EVEN BETTER: Emotional outbursts are almost invariably a matter of our losing perspective. Unfortunately, the workplace, with its sundry pressures and pettiness, is quite prone to such a loss. You can try to maintain a more calm perspective by slowing down, taking a few deep breaths, looking out the window, taking a short break—and also by taking a long-range view: most of the things that we get bent out of shape about are quickly forgotten within a few days or weeks. So why waste all that energy?

RULE FIFTY-SIX
KEEP IT SHORT AND SWEET

If you do a Google search for job interview tips, the advice to not ramble will pop up time and time again—but it's not just good advice for interviews. It's applicable to the rest of your professional life as well.

WHAT IT MEANS: In two words: don't ramble. Answer the question, or make your point, clearly and succinctly—and then stop. Overlong, rambling answers can make you sound apologetic, nervous, or indecisive. It's better to leave them wanting more than wishing you had talked less.

ACTION PLAN: Familiarizing yourself as much as possible with your speech (or the remarks you intend to make) will help keep you from getting off track. Be sensitive to the notion of providing too much information. If people want to know additional details, they will ask. Above all, avoid the tendency to repeat yourself—that's when you'll start to lose your audience. As a favorite public speaker of mine says, "If you don't strike oil after twenty minutes, stop boring!"

EVEN BETTER: Most of us have a natural fear of "dead air"—that uncomfortable silence in the room (even in a one-to-one conversation) after we have said something. That's why many of us try to fill it with words. The best way to overcome your discomfort with dead air is to practice—and to become more comfortable with the silent gaps in conversation. Believe it or not, it will make you appear more thoughtful, more serious, and more in control. Hey, it worked during the job interview, didn't it?

RULE FIFTY-SEVEN
ZIG WHEN OTHERS ZAG

If you follow the pack, you will probably never do what it takes to lead the pack. What's worse, you may be left way behind. The strategic remedy? Do something different—not just a little different, but dramatically different. Like the big, high-profile razzle-dazzle play in football, it just could make your market stand up and cheer.

WHAT IT MEANS: The essence of effective marketing is positioning your products or services so that they stand out above and beyond your competition. Part of the challenge in achieving this is to get noticed—to create, through your packaging, advertising, and branding, a more *outstanding* impression. One way to do this is to zig when others zag. For example, look no further than the cereal box aisle in your supermarket. It's a motley mix of one bold, colorful, eye-catching package after another—but it's too noisy, because they are all fighting for your attention in a similar way. What if there was a cereal with black-and-white or sepia-toned packaging? Wouldn't that make a dramatic contrast against the sea of colors? That's zigging when others zag. There's no guarantee that it will always work, but it's always worth considering.

ACTION PLAN: Develop your own sense of "zig." Look for ads, packaging, marketing strategies, et cetera, that are dynamically different. What is it about them that makes them truly outstanding? This can open you up to new possibilities—and to creating the kind of "breakthrough marketing" that can yield more dramatic results. These days, with e-mail marketing, interactive ads, and "secret agent" marketing (hired guns talking up the new product in a seemingly chance encounter), there are more possibilities than ever.

EVEN BETTER: Develop a "zig" strategy component in all your marketing planning—something truly out of the box. Maybe even something that was never in the box. You should then evaluate its potential risks and rewards against other plans, but at least give your zig option its due consideration. It just could lead to the Big Idea you need to propel your business to the next level.

RULE FIFTY-EIGHT
CRITICIZE CONSTRUCTIVELY

Is constructive criticism a contradiction in terms? Certainly not! It may, however, be one of the most difficult things you'll have to do as a manager or business owner. Criticizing constructively can elevate, motivate, and help people's performance be more aligned with your expectations. It's an opportunity to reinforce relationships, not trash them—but you need to know how to do it right.

WHAT IT MEANS: Realize that whenever you need to criticize someone, you are treading on thin ice—people tend to be defensive when criticized and can create elaborate rationalizations that would surely strain almost anyone else's belief. Never criticize anyone when you feel angry, insulted, or wronged. Never criticize in public. Never criticize in an emotional or accusatory way. Finally, focus on the deed, not the doer—on what happened rather than what the person did. If you can avoid the word *you* all together, you are probably on the right track.

ACTION PLAN: Be prepared before you call someone on the carpet. What exactly do you want to discuss? Paint a clear picture of what you expect in the future. Take the time to ask the person to explain his or her side of the story. There may be more to the picture than meets your eye. Also, insist that the person commit to doing what needs to be done to fix the mistake or prevent it from happening again. Understanding what to do and getting a commitment to do it should be your two goals.

EVEN BETTER: Let the other person suggest the remedy. Ask what it will take to keep this from happening again. Finally, end on an upbeat note. Thank the person for cooperating, express your optimism about the future, and let the employee know that his or her efforts are still very much appreciated.

RULE FIFTY-NINE
BE READY TO PLAY PEACEMAKER

Mediating a conflict is challenging, but as a manager or supervisor, the role of mediator comes with your territory. Your willingness to appropriately intervene sets the stage for your own success. You craft a work environment that enables the success of the people who work there. Like so many other skills, conflict mediation is an example of practice makes perfect.

WHAT IT MEANS: Organization leaders are responsible for creating a work environment that enables people to thrive. If turf wars, disagreements, and differences of opinion escalate into interpersonal conflict, you must intervene immediately. Not intervening is not an option if you value your organization and your positive culture. In conflict-ridden situations, your mediation skill and interventions are critical. Above all, do not avoid the conflict, hoping it will go away—that's wishful thinking at its worst.

An unresolved conflict or interpersonal disagreement festers just under the surface in your work environment. It rises to the surface whenever enabled, and always at the worst possible moment.

ACTION PLAN: Meet with the antagonists together. Let each briefly summarize his or her point of view, without comment or interruption by the other party. This should be a short discussion so that all parties are clear about the disagreement and conflicting views. Intervene if either employee attacks the other employee. This is not acceptable.

Ask each participant to describe specific actions he or she would like to see the other party take that would resolve the differences. For example, Tom may feel that he needs to have full responsibility for managing the Oswald account because the current division of labor is causing him too much difficulty in tracking and expediting that client's projects.

Sometimes, you as the manager may have to establish a new procedure or process to resolve the conflict. The key question to ask: what about the work situation is causing these staff members to fail?

EVEN BETTER: If the situation needs further exploration, here's a conflict resolution technique recommended by Stephen Covey: ask each participant to additionally identify what the other employee can do more of, less of, stop, and start. Above all, fight clean!

It is okay to have reasonable disagreements over issues and plans; it is never okay to have personality conflicts that affect the workplace.

RULE SIXTY
NEW DAY, NEW ANSWER

You can call them challenges, problems, or opportunities in disguise—but every manager and every business owner must resolve these issues: how to compete more effectively in the marketplace, how to retain more customers, how to design systems that enable people to monitor and manage more effectively. And there's one more problem you can almost certainly add to the mix: the problem of inertia.

WHAT IT MEANS: Markets change. Technology changes. Competition changes.

Most people today probably can't even begin to imagine doing business without computers or a fax machine—much less a cell phone—yet once upon a time, that's exactly how businesses operated. In order to move your business ahead, you have to avoid the tendency of getting stuck in the past. If it isn't broke, don't fix it—but stay alert for products, systems, and anything else that may not be working as well as they once did and consider new answers. Or as a clever business associate of mine likes to say, "Business as usual isn't."

ACTION PLAN: Have everyone list at least three things about your business that most need to be to changed. What should those changes be? Those items that are most frequently indicated will point you in the right direction.

EVEN BETTER: Expose yourself to new developments and possibilities within your industry and beyond and consider how they might benefit your organization. Also look for shifts in consumer attitudes as reflected in hot new products. You can ride the wave of a buying trend all the way to the bank—but only if you spot it early and respond swiftly.

RULE SIXTY-ONE
BE A SAVVY NEWS CONSUMER

It's easy to become so focused on your business that everything else seems irrelevant, but businesses function in the real world—and so should you! Keeping yourself well informed on current events can broaden your perspective. Being interested in a wide range of topics (and people) can make you a more interesting person—and interesting people generally have more interesting ideas, not to mention a more extensive network of contacts.

WHAT IT MEANS: Don't dwell on your business or professional role to the exclusion of everything else. That's not commitment—it's obsession. One remedy is to broaden your perspective, and one good way to regularly detach from your all-business focus is to read the newspaper. Obviously, you should stay in touch with news and trends in your industry, but you need to be able to make small talk once in a while too. For instance, you don't need to read the sports pages every day, but you should know who's in the World Series, Super Bowl, or NBA finals. Maybe you'll learn about a new movie or restaurant to go to. Maybe an article in the business section will spark a smart idea. There's only one good way to find out—read all about it!

ACTION PLAN: If you don't read a newspaper, start. If you do, start skimming through those sections that you usually skip. You may or may not find yourself developing a new interest, but you'll become better informed in more areas than you are now. Being "topically diverse" is good for your brain—and learning more about virtually anything is good for you.

EVEN BETTER: Check out news magazines or magazines or news Web sites that you usually don't read. If you want to think outside the box, sometimes you have to read outside the box. Reading is a wonderful way to expose yourself to new ideas, to develop new interests, and to open the door to new possibilities. After all, isn't that why you're reading this book?

DON'T HAVE RULES
JUST TO HAVE RULES

Every business has its rules, policies, and procedures—the way things are done. It could be the procedure for filing an expense report, the way a new customer is registered on your computer system, or how many paid sick days an employee may receive each year. Most of the time (let's assume), these policies make sense. Sometimes, though, they get in the way. And that's like having the tail wag the dog.

WHAT IT MEANS: Policies stop making sense when they interfere with the key objectives of your business—are you losing sales, customers, or valued employees because of them? There might be new technologies, practices, or processes that could result in greater efficiency or more strategically valuable information for managers. Or perhaps the rule or procedure simply fails to achieve its original objective and is being followed for no good reason at all. There are hundreds of opportunities to fine-tune and improve any company's performance—but weeding out your dumb or dysfunctional rules is a great place to start!

ACTION PLAN: Periodically review all policies, processes, and rules. Do they still make sense? Are there any modifications that might make more sense? Those employees who are closest to the operational processes may very well have better insight into possible rules remedies, so make sure to invite their feedback.

EVEN BETTER: Empower everyone in the company to be in the position of making constructive suggestions. You can implement a formal "Suggestion Box" program with rewards and recognition, or you could form a special Operations Committee to make policy reviews a more formal and regularly conducted activity. The more flexible your business can be with regard to continually improving its practices and operating procedures, the more agile and successful your company will be.

RULE SIXTY-THREE
RECOGNIZE ENTREPRENEURIAL TYPES

Some people thrive on autonomy and can get things done with minimal supervision, whereas others are more comfortable with being given specific directions and a greater sense of structure. Being able to manage each type of employee for optimal results requires flexibility as well as an ability to discern these two very different types of worker.

WHAT IT MEANS: Treating every worker equally does not mean that you have to treat every worker the same. Those who truly have an entrepreneurial bent (self-managing, resourceful, able to solve problems independently) can do more for you—if you give them the opportunity. Similarly, nonentrepreneurial types will be more likely to thrive in situations where the "rules" and contingencies are clearly delineated—with ready access to a supervisor for any clarification or problem solving that might be needed. Adjust your managerial style accordingly, and everyone benefits.

ACTION PLAN: Find out who your budding entrepreneurs are by throwing out some long-term goals and challenges to your workgroup and inviting input on a strictly optional basis—kind of like an extra-credit project. Some workers will have some answers right on the spot. Others will get back to you with some recommendations that might be well worth considering. Those workers who opt out or can't complete this task without asking a slew of questions are more likely to fit the "worker bee" profile—and be more likely to excel in a meticulously defined job role.

EVEN BETTER: Brainstorm with the entrepreneurial types to develop a consensus solution, and then empower this team (or its most impressive member) to write up the proposal and either implement it or present it for senior management's consideration. Entrepreneurs respond well to challenges, so challenge them: what would it take from you (or senior management) to implement the new plan?

RULE SIXTY-FOUR
CORNER THE UNCONTESTED MARKET

Very few companies sell services or products that are truly unique. However, if you're offering the only product of its kind being sold in a store (or any sales channel), it has the clear advantages of being more distinctive in its setting by virtue of the fact that it is not competing with any similar type of product. It is, in effect, a "micromonopoly"—an uncontested market.

WHAT IT MEANS: Let's say you manufacture an elegant line of pocket knives. You sell pocket knives into all the markets that your competition does— in drugstores and hardware stores, in catalogs, and on your own Web site. What if you could introduce your pocket knives into a retail channel where no pocket knives have been sold before—a convenience store, perhaps, or jewelry stores?

ACTION PLAN: Bring your notebook with you for an entire week as you visit various retail stores. Look at what's being sold and offered. Can you conceive of any place that might make sense as an uncontested market? For example, you might consider selling sunglasses in a tennis or golf shop—or in fashion boutiques. You might be able to sell books on tennis (or a tennis video) to that tennis shop. Or in-store monogramming equipment. Or…?

EVEN BETTER: Be on the lookout for products and services in uncontested markets wherever you go. You may be quite surprised at how many things are available outside their normal retail channels. And it could help you establish some brave, new, and—for the moment—competition-free sales possibilities of your own.

RULE SIXTY-FIVE
Don't Lose Your Sense of Humor

When the going gets tough, smart managers lighten up. Recent studies show that a sense of humor is the most consistent characteristic among executives promoted in major companies, and that managers showing a sense of humor advance faster and further than those without one.

WHAT IT MEANS: Humor promotes creative thinking, mental flexibility, and the ability to cope with change—and that's what our lives are full of. In expressing confidence and building it in others, humor is invaluable. The right funny comment at just the right time shows a grasp of the situation like nothing else. Self-effacing humor is especially good for expressing confidence. When you poke fun at your own shortcomings, you show that you can face problems squarely, without defensive illusions. Most of all, laughter restores the gift of perspective, making our troubles appear to be much less daunting, and our fears much less formidable. Adhering to this rule does not mean that you should be a joker or the office clown. Kidding around too much can undercut your professionalism. Your guideline: take the work seriously, but don't take yourself so seriously.

ACTION PLAN: Do what you can to lighten up your work atmosphere. Spontaneous wit is probably preferable to rehearsed shtick, but do whatever feels comfortable to you. Keep the humor gentle and avoid making fun of people—some people won't mind, but some will. Some offices are minefields of sarcasm and cynicism—don't let yours be one of them. Share a funny office-related incident. Begin your presentation with an apt joke or clever quote. Hang up a parody motivational poster (*www.despair.com* has some of the best). The workplace abounds with comic material, and you don't have to be a stand-up comic to harvest it.

EVEN BETTER: Send the signal that it's OK for everyone to express their sense of humor—within reasonable limits. As a manager, your behavior can set the tone for others to follow. By making and allowing humorous comments (and the best feedback of all is a genuine laugh), you'll be sending the signal to your colleagues that it's OK not to be "soooooo serious"—as long as the work gets done. And that's no joke!

Be Direct about What You Really Want

Salespeople might recognize this as a corollary of the cardinal rule "Ask for the sale."

The underlying principle is indeed quite similar. You can make a dazzling presentation—to a customer, your boss, your committee, whomever—but if you don't include a clear and compelling call to action, you are omitting the most critical element.

WHAT IT MEANS: Most people have a certain resistance to making specific requests because it's a bit risky. Maybe you'll be rejected. Maybe you're afraid to be perceived as too pushy. But this is one discomfort you will have to work to overcome. Look at it this way: if you don't ask for what you want, who will? The good news is, if you are clear and at ease about asking for what you want, you may be pleasantly surprised at how often you get it. Successful salespeople know full well that the presentation is just a prelude to "the close," and so should you.

ACTION PLAN: Be clear and articulate about what you want from your next meeting—and ask for it! Rehearse aloud, so you can neutralize the fear factor. Anticipate objections and develop good replies. Invite feedback from your personal support group. As with any presentation, preparation and practice are key. Also, take a more positive view of rejection. "No" might mean "not now." No sales pros—even the superstars—get the order every time.

EVEN BETTER: Keep asking! If at first you don't receive … ask and ask again! Situations change, and selling anything (including your ideas) is not so much an event as a process, so keep the process going—with follow-up calls, e-mails, et cetera. The more often you ask for what you want, the more likely you'll get it.

RULE SIXTY-SEVEN
GIVE PEOPLE CHOICES

You wouldn't walk into a clothing store and expect to see only two or three suits or dresses, would you? As a consumer, you expect choices. *P.S.:* So does everyone else! The original Model-T Ford sold in only one model and one color, which was fine until the car industry became more competitive. If your industry is competitive, you'll be more successful if you offer people more choices too.

WHAT IT MEANS: Offering more choices—not just in products, colors, and styles,

but also in range of services, delivery options, and payment terms—makes it easier for customers to buy from you for two reasons: you're increasing your probability of meeting their needs or preferences, and you're making it easier to do business. For example, on eBay, there are some vendors who will accept only a money order or a cashier's check whereas others accept PayPal and all major credit cards. All other things being equal, which vendor would you choose?

ACTION PLAN: Scout your competition—and even companies in related industries—for ideas on how you might expand and diversify your product selection or service offerings. Are other companies offering more flexible terms that you could emulate? Make sure to get positive feedback from current customers, focus groups, et cetera, before proceeding to a full-scale rollout.

EVEN BETTER: Factor more choices into your product-development plans. For example, if you're a product manufacturer, consider offering an economy model, a standard model, and a deluxe model. There is safety in diversification—and often a greater opportunity for profit.

RULE SIXTY-EIGHT
BE THE EARLY BIRD

It's true what they say about the early bird catching the worm. It's been said (by Woody Allen) that 80 percent of life is just showing up, then another 10 percent may be getting there first. Beginning projects ASAP is one of the best strategies around for getting things done on time—and that's a good thing for any professional's reputation.

WHAT IT MEANS: Whether you're driving to Aunt Louise's for Thanksgiving dinner or polishing up that marketing plan, things tend to take longer than planned. The smart solution: start earlier. This allows you more "wiggle room" when the inevitable glitches and snarls occur, which will very likely save you the drama and agita of sweating out yet another down-to-the-wire deadline. Another plus: there can often be some resistance to starting anything new, and that's understandable. The principle of inertia isn't just for physics. Nevertheless, procrastination doesn't really work—whereas getting an early jump on a project will. The very act of beginning something gives it a momentum all its own.

ACTION PLAN: Begin something now. It doesn't have to be an assigned project, just something work-related that you've been meaning to do. See what happens. Repeat as needed. Starting things early is almost like giving yourself extra time—and that's one of the most precious gifts of all.

EVEN BETTER: Don't just start early—finish early! You'll lose some of your stress, feel more on top of things, and develop a twenty-four-karat reputation as someone who not only gets things done, but does so well ahead of schedule. People like that get noticed—and promoted.

THE GOLDEN RULE
SHOULD APPLY IN BUSINESS

Sometimes it may be necessary for you to criticize or even reprimand someone. Sometimes you may be angry at what someone did (or didn't do), and be quite ready to inflict your wrath. All of this can be done in a stern yet professional way—but there is never any need to be cruel. Even if you can get away with it, you should stay away from it. It's not just the right thing to do; it's a more professional way to behave—and to do business.

WHAT IT MEANS: The Golden Rule doesn't lapse at your company's door. In other words, strive to treat your subordinates the way you would want to be treated if your roles were reversed. Most people do not appreciate being ridiculed or abused by their boss. They may fear it, and they may even respond to it, but they won't respect it. Toxic bosses create toxic workplaces—demoralized workplaces where the top priorities become placating Mr. Blowhard and covering one's flank. Turnover, fear, and loathing ensue—none of which serve your business very well.

ACTION PLAN: Manage with your head, not your hormones. Do not give yourself permission to treat anyone cruelly. The next time you sense your anger shift into overdrive and start to bubble over onto a subordinate or coworker, just STOP. Take a deep breath. And give yourself a time-out. It's perfectly OK to say, "You know, I am so ticked off at you right now that I don't even want to talk about this, so I'm going to give myself a few minutes to cool down and we can discuss this later." What if you're the victim of a tyrannically abusive boss? Unless you've adopted an effective coping strategy (and it is quite possible that there is none), my advice to you would be to seek employment elsewhere while your dignity and self-respect are still relatively intact.

EVEN BETTER: Strive to create a workplace where respect and common courtesy prevail. If you're the boss, people will model themselves after your behavior. If you're a manager, you can consistently and firmly indicate your position on anger management and zero tolerance of abusive behavior by members of your workgroup or team. In the stressful business world, there will inevitably be some emotional fireworks and flare-ups, and that's tolerable. You don't have to referee every argument or confrontation, but like a good referee, you should remind your "fighters" to fight "clean"—and you should not hesitate to step in and separate them if they don't.

RULE SEVENTY
LOCATION ISN'T JUST ABOUT REAL ESTATE

Although it's often taken for granted, the physical, aesthetic, and ergonomic components of your workplace can affect morale and productivity. Cluttered, crowded, grungy offices, with people having to squeeze around each other in narrow hallways, add a significant load to everyone's "stressometer."

WHAT IT MEANS: Strive to offer your employees—and yourself—a comfortable, clean, and even attractive office environment that exhibits the company pride you would expect from your workers. Are the lighting and ventilation and office furniture up to par? Is there sufficient storage? When people look at the walls, will they notice interesting art or peeling paint? Such human-comfort factors are often avoided during the start-up phase of a business in favor of "pursuing the dream," but once there are more people on board and enough operating capital to move your business off Mom's folding table, you do need to design a workspace that works for you, not against you.

ACTION PLAN: Add some plants and some office art, and encourage employees to add personal touches to their work areas. Consider little amenities—like coat closets, a company bulletin board, or desktop lamps. An office should not be a static place; it should change and evolve regularly.

EVEN BETTER: Develop a wish list of office upgrade ideas (new furniture, expanded storage capability, office art collection, remodeled reception area, etc.) and budget for it. Prioritize on the basis of urgency of need and/or potential value. Investing in the look and feel of your workplace is not just cosmetic—it says something about the professionalism and stability of your company, and even more, that you're committed to giving your people the kind of people-friendly workplace that's more conducive to success.

RULE SEVENTY-ONE
MAKE SURE TO HAVE AT
LEAST ONE SPECIALTY

Of course it's good to know a little bit about everything and to be as familiar as possible with every aspect of your business—but you don't want your knowledge base to be a mile wide and an inch deep. Becoming an expert in a strategically relevant area or two can greatly enhance your current value to your company— and be a valuable selling point throughout your career.

WHAT IT MEANS: Although you will probably be expected to be a "generalist" as a manager, it pays to acquire a specialty. For example, if you're a marketing manager, you might learn about how to export to European countries or about direct mail or about database marketing techniques. Having this specialty can help your business pursue promising opportunities that it might otherwise have not considered.

ACTION PLAN: Consider an area or two of interest that you could develop further as your professional specialty, and then get educated. These days you have many options: books, seminars, online research, or, possibly, being apprenticed to a mentor. Use any or all methods as needed. Your company may, ideally, subsidize the cost of a course or seminar, but don't let that become an obstacle. Dig into your own pocket if you have to. It's tax deductible—and it's worth it!

EVEN BETTER: Once you have developed your expertise, you need to put it into play. This will require some self-marketing. Let the powers that be know of your expertise. Suggest or volunteer for projects that would utilize it. One great way of establishing yourself as an expert is to write an article and get it published or widely circulated. Presenting at a conference can also solidify your credentials as an expert.

RULE SEVENTY-TWO
KNOW YOUR TECHNOLOGY

You don't need to adopt every new business gadget that comes down the pike, but you should be aware of them. Knowledge is power—and knowledge of what's new and could potentially improve your company's productivity and efficiency can be powerfully profitable.

WHAT IT MEANS: There's a certain resistance to adopting new technology. Very few people today would question the indispensable value of calculators, copiers, or computers, yet not everyone jumped on the bandwagon when these tools were first made available. Part of the reason may have been a high price tag, but another key factor was just plain old inertia: "This is the way it's always been done. If it ain't broke, don't fix it." Nonsense! There's a window of opportunity between the early adopters of a new technology and when the rest of the world jumps on the bandwagon—and that window could give you a significant boost over your competition.

ACTION PLAN: Stay in touch with what's ahead of the curve by asking tech-savvy friends, reading business news and newsmagazines, and scouting the exhibit booths at trade shows. If you have a friend or associate who's raving about his or her latest business toy, treat it as an opportunity to learn some potentially useful information. Believe me, people who are enamored with their shiny new high-tech gizmo are usually more than delighted to talk about it.

EVEN BETTER: To take things to the next level, learn a little bit about how the new technology works. Your goal is not to become the tech support guy or official office geek, but simply to become a more well-informed consumer—if and when you do decide to obtain the new device. Better yet: comprehensively consider (and get others in your business to consider) the product's potential impact on your business. Do the pros outweigh the cons?

RULE SEVENTY-THREE
HIRE SLOWLY; HIRE WELL

Great employees are often hard to find—but it's worth taking the time and making the effort. Don't settle for second-rate. And don't give in to the understandable temptation (and operational urgency) to fill an open position as soon as possible.

WHAT IT MEANS: It's probably one of the most mouthed corporate clichés of all time, but it has the virtue of being true: your people *are* your most valuable asset. Every new hire is an opportunity to add to the value and long-term strength of your business—but only if you do it right. A superstar candidate will make your job easier and improve your capabilities in ways you may not even realize until they happen. This is one critical aspect of managing a business that should be deliberate and deadline-free.

ACTION PLAN: Cast a wider net by advertising in more places. Ask your own employees for qualified referrals (some companies offer incentives for referrals that result in a hire). Put the word out through your own extended network. Sharpen your interviewing skills. And don't dwell exclusively on related experience. Although it's a significant factor, so are personality traits and chemistry. You want reliability. You want a person whom you can "click with" every day. And most of all, you want to be genuinely impressed by that person's track record and/or potential.

EVEN BETTER: For senior positions, consider using an executive recruiter. You will pay handsomely for this service, but it will help you reach high-caliber candidates (perhaps those working for your direct competitors) who may not even be actively searching for a new career opportunity.

GET NEW EMPLOYEES OFF TO A GOOD START

Most companies spend a fraction of the time and effort to orient new employees that they do to recruit them. That's a mistake. With the right kind of training and treatment, your orientation process can make a good first-day impression on your employee—and vice versa. You'll have less turnover and probably get new employees up to speed more rapidly.

WHAT IT MEANS: The hiring process doesn't end with making the selection. Your new employee's first day is critical. People are most motivated on their first day. Build on the momentum of that motivation by having a place set up for them to work, making them comfortable, and making them feel welcome. Don't just dump them in an office and shut your door. Be prepared to spend some time with them, explaining job duties, getting them started on tasks, or even taking them out to lunch. By doing so, you're building rapport and setting the stage for a long and happy working relationship.

ACTION PLAN: Develop a formal orientation plan. This should include welcoming the new hires personally and making sure that you (or their manager) spend some time with them. Go over some of the job's specific responsibilities and some basic workplace rules. Provide any reference material that might be useful.

EVEN BETTER: Make sure that new hires are introduced in person to all their immediate coworkers (and give them a list). Send a memo to your staff to announce the new hire. Add some fun to the experience by treating the rookie the lunch.

RULE SEVENTY-FIVE
IT'S ALL IN THE DELIVERY

The right words, tone, mood, time, et cetera can affect how well your message gets across—or doesn't. All too often, the first thing that pops into your head could benefit from revision.

WHAT IT MEANS: There's a time where humor or sarcasm might be appropriate, but if you happen to be criticizing someone's performance, it's probably not the time. There's a time when you can be more jovial and lighthearted, and other times when you have to be the more buttoned-up "Ms. Serious Manager." It's always important to be sensitive to how you say something and not just what you say. Venting your anger or making a withering remark might feel good at the moment, but you may regret your uninhibited outburst for many days afterward. Stay cool!

ACTION PLAN: Couple criticism with praise. Nobody really likes being criticized, but everyone does appreciate being treated with sensitivity and respect. When you do have to call someone to task, do it seriously, specifically, and on an even keel emotionally. Temper the criticism by letting the employee know that you are satisfied with his or her work quality overall, that this is just one thing (albeit an important one) that needs to be corrected, and that you are confident in his or her ability to do so. As the saying goes, you can catch more flies with honey than with vinegar.

EVEN BETTER: As much as possible, take the time to consider how you will say something. Also, people tend to communicate more effectively when they're in a positive frame of mind, so make sure that frame fits you. If you're perturbed, enraged, surly, frustrated, annoyed—or in any other subpar emotional state—wait for it to pass or at least subside before reprimanding, criticizing, or confronting someone.

Let Your Word Be Your Bond ... and Your Reputation

When it comes to business agreements, your word or handshake should be your bond. Make sure to earn and maintain a reputation for honoring your agreements.

WHAT IT MEANS: These days, everything is documented to the max for legal and security precautions—and certainly it's good to have all the i's dotted and the t's crossed—but don't let the tail wag the dog. If you and your counterpart have basically agreed to something, don't allow the deal to fall apart over trivialities and technicalities. If the agreement is one you can live with, then make it a done deal ASAP.

ACTION PLAN: Act as if the deal were done. Place an order. Do the very next thing you can do to work toward sealing the deal. In other words, start living up to your end of the deal—and do so with a sense of urgency. Why? Because deals have a certain momentum, and I've seen quite a few business deals die because of bureaucratic inertia. Once you've given your word—or handshake—you owe it to your reputation (and your company's) to make your agreement a fait accompli.

EVEN BETTER: As soon as possible following your agreement, send an e-mail to your counterpart summarizing its main points. This will help ensure that you are on the same page and seal the deal. It might even make life a little easier for the lawyers—not that there's anything wrong with that.

RULE SEVENTY-SEVEN
YOUR COWORKERS ARE MORE THAN JUST NAMES

Your coworkers have lives outside the office. Without being a busybody, it's good to show an interest in them as people. Appreciating the fact that people are more than their jobs and responding accordingly is an intangible but genuine "environmental upgrade" that doesn't cost a penny and can help build more cohesive work teams.

WHAT IT MEANS: Although you want to be serious and businesslike, all work and no small talk makes Jack or Jane incredibly tedious to work with. The human element is often neglected in the workplace—and certainly the focus should be on the work, but not exclusively. Office-cooler chitchat has its role in forging smoother working relationships and simply adding a more human (and humane) element to office life. As a boss or supervisor, you don't want to get too buddy-buddy, but you don't want to come across as a cold automaton either.

ACTION PLAN: Show some interest in your coworkers. How's their family? What did they do over the weekend? What interests and activities do they pursue after hours? If you're genuinely interested, people will usually respond positively (of course, if it's not your m.o., they may be understandably suspicious or startled at first). A little bit of small talk is good grease for the wheels of commerce. Make sure to avoid such potentially divisive topics as politics or religion or offensive jokes. Also, don't forget to celebrate birthdays and special personal occasions. You don't have to plan the details of these office events, but make sure to authorize and participate in them.

EVEN BETTER: Getting a little more personal is a two-way street—so make sure that your coworkers get to know a little more about you. One good way to do this: have lunch with coworkers from time to time and make sure that the topics of conversation are not all business.

You Can't Put "Thank You" in the Bank

This rule is tricky because it's a bit of a balancing act and a judgment call. To woo a client, you naturally want to put your best foot forward. You want to be as helpful as possible so as to demonstrate your expertise or the quality of your product or service. And that's OK—but that said, don't let visions of monster orders seduce you into giving away the store.

WHAT IT MEANS: At some point—and the sooner, the better—you have to start getting paid. After all, you are trying to stay in business. There are some customers who will think nothing of stringing you along with promises, buck-passing, delays, et cetera, and sometimes that's a legitimate part of the sales cycle. It's a little bit like fishing—you have to know when to give a little more line and when to cut bait.

ACTION PLAN: Review all the times you've been strung along by a customer. Did you have a sense at any time that you were being taken advantage of? In retrospect, what could you have done to avoid or curtail that scenario? Also realize that many people (and yes, customers are people) will take whatever they think they can get away with, so it's up to you to set limits and to say no.

EVEN BETTER: Discuss this issue with your sales manager or more experienced sales reps. Different companies will take different positions on this issue—and a certain amount of discretion is well advised. For example, a potentially HUGE customer might be worth a little more leeway. Nevertheless, it is generally a good idea to make it clear to your prospects that they can get a sample or an initial consultation or a detailed proposal but that the meter will start running at Point A. Ask for the sale!

TEST YOUR HUNCHES

You or your team members will almost surely have intriguing new ideas about how to market your products, improve your operations, or otherwise grow your business. Some of them will probably pay off—but you don't know that up front. Never bet the farm (or you career) on a hunch, no matter how slam-dunk sure you feel about it. Follow the prudent course: test!

WHAT IT MEANS: If you take a seat-of-your-pants approach to implementing every promising idea, you could wind up falling on ... the seat of your pants. Testing is a smart and more professional way to reality-check the soundness of virtually any innovation. Of course, tests aren't foolproof. They may not eliminate all of the risk, but they do reduce it. And, if the test results suggest that the idea is not worth pursuing, it can save you a bundle.

ACTION PLAN: Consider how you might be able to test your next hunch. At the very least, actively seek the critical feedback of others. They may have reservations, insights, and perspectives that don't occur to you. Direct mail is especially amenable to testing, allowing you to test such critical components as offers, lists, packages (including design and copy), and timing (when you mail) on a limited basis before "rolling it out" to your targeted market.

EVEN BETTER: Do your homework by conducting surveys and focus groups, or by acquiring relevant market research to bolster your hunch. Many companies have adapted the software industry's practice of "beta testers" and have assembled groups of customers who are willing to try potential new products in exchange for their detailed feedback. In general, the more empirical evidence that you can gather to support that your hunch is worthwhile, the more likely your hunch will prove to indeed be worthwhile.

RULE EIGHTY
If You Think You'll Fail, You Probably Will

Abraham Lincoln once said, "Whether you think you can or think you can't, you're probably right." Well, he was probably right. Your attitude can greatly determine your altitude (how far you will go), so make sure that you're not holding yourself back by the constraints of your own mind.

WHAT IT MEANS: Your attitude and interior monologue (self-talk) can help you succeed or persuade you to feel like a miserable, incompetent, and unworthy loser—but guess what? You can change the tape. Positive thinking may not change the world, but it can change your world. You don't have to be a mystic or a mental marshmallow to do this—just take a closer look at what you're telling yourself … and be more aware of the toxic "life sucks" attitude that might be emanating from your coworkers, because people like that have it exactly backward: negative attitudes have a way of sucking the life out of any endeavor.

ACTION PLAN: Examine your own attitudes and self-talk. Are you generally a positive, pleasant person, or are you more fearful, resentful, or cynical? Are there any attitudes that you feel may be getting in the way of your personal or professional fulfillment? Make it a priority to reprogram your "inner tapes" and to bring more optimism into your life. What will it take to do that?

EVEN BETTER: Workplaces can be quite negative too—but you don't have to add to the mess. Instead, resolve to deal with abusive people and other emotional black holes more adroitly—by not getting so ensnared in their drama, by setting boundaries, and by being more assertive. As a manager or boss, you can also send the signal that such negativity is about as welcome in your workplace as cigarette smoke—because it can be even more hazardous to a healthy office environment.

KEEP YOUR ROLODEX UP TO DATE

By "Rolodex," I may be indicating my age, but I mean any place where you keep your contact information, whether on cards, your Palm, or your PC. People move on. Numbers change. And you may simply neglect to enter new contacts—only to regret that fact when you urgently need to contact them.

WHAT IT MEANS: Your Rolodex is the key to your personal/professional network—everyone you know and might call upon one day with a question or for a favor or in regard to getting something done. And, like any valuable tool, it needs to be kept in good working condition. That means having accurate information (phone number, cell phone number, fax number, e-mail address, real-world address, how you know them, what they do, etc.) as well as continually and comprehensively adding new contacts as you make them. When adding to your Rolodex, you want to cast as wide a net as possible, because you never know who you might want or need to call. It's better to have the number on file and not need it than to need it and not have it.

ACTION PLAN: Get into the habit of collecting names and numbers for most of the people you meet, both socially and in the course of your business day. This practice alone can give you the advantage of a fatter Rolodex and might encourage you to be more outgoing—a characteristic that can contribute significantly to your success. Try to add the new contact ASAP, or keep a file where new business cards and contact info can be stored until you can enter the data.

EVEN BETTER: Include useful notes that might help jog your memory. How did you meet this person? What does she do? Where did you meet? Basically, anything that can help you place the person in some meaningful context is potentially useful. Sometimes you will need to pick up the phone or shoot an e-mail to someone whom you haven't connected to in quite some time, and at those times, having some context data on file can make the difference between having a contact and having the name and number of a complete stranger.

RULE EIGHTY-TWO
Don't Dwell on the Past

We're all carrying emotional baggage—the residual pain, guilt, anger, shame, regret, et cetera, over past mistakes, setbacks, and other painful learning experiences—but it's better to check that baggage at the office door. It will only weigh you down.

WHAT IT MEANS: Too much living in the past can impede your present. Learn from your mistakes or other difficult life experiences, sure—but then move on. The more emotionally entangled you are with the past, the more it rents space in your head—and that's space (and mental energy) that can be put to much better use. Being present-focused is a more constructive, productive, and satisfying way to work—and to live.

ACTION PLAN: Realize that you have the capability of changing your thoughts in the blink of an eye. The next time you're all wrapped up in "woulda, coulda, shoulda," make an effort to be aware of your "past mode" and mentally shift gears. You can literally tell yourself (aloud, if nobody's within earshot), "Not now!" or "I will think about this in three hours!" or even "That was then, this is now." You may not be able to manage all your thoughts, but once you discover that it is at least possible to shift thoughts—and to be more cognizant of them—you will be more in the driver's seat.

And then, as with any new skill, all you have to do is practice.

EVEN BETTER: There's an old saying: when life gives you lemons, make lemonade.

To diffuse the emotional fallout of past setbacks, resentments, and/ or disappointments, try to reframe them. Did you learn anything from the experience? Was there any "upside" at all? With the benefit of time and a more dispassionate perspective, some of our most challenging life experiences can be reviewed as some of our life's most essential lessons.

RULE EIGHTY-THREE
CHECK YOUR EGO AT THE DOOR

It's good to be confident in yourself and your abilities. It's good to have professional pride and to do everything you can to maintain your good reputation, but too many managers and business owners let their egos run roughshod over their employees—and, perhaps even more harmfully, over their own good judgment.

WHAT IT MEANS: An unchecked ego will, sooner or later, be bad for business. It leads to impulsive, ill-considered, and capriciously authoritative decisions ("Do this because I say so!"), and is a poor substitute for objectively considering the facts. More than a few companies' primary operating principle is to do whatever makes the boss happy, not necessarily what's best for the business. The two are not always the same. On a personal level, our ego may lead us to suspect that we are right all the time or that we are far more talented than the mere mortals around us or that we are entitled to an endless stream of praise and adoration. When you start acting as if any of these ego-inflated assumptions are correct, problems will ensue. The fact is that everyone else in your business has an ego too—and if you want respect, you have to give respect. Three simple words to always keep in mind: get over yourself!

ACTION PLAN: Honestly review those times in your career when your ego worked to your disadvantage. What might you do differently the next time? Another good question to ask yourself: am I more focused on the work or myself?

EVEN BETTER: Don't let your ego drive your demeanor or your decision making. Be open to the possibility that other people are worth listening to. Be respectful of other people, and make sure to stroke their egos from time to time as merited. Finally, become more attuned to the ever-present ego currents and undercurrents in your workplace. This is one critical people skill that will be of great benefit to any manager.

RULE EIGHTY-FOUR

THE CUSTOMER IS
NOT ALWAYS RIGHT

Other rules in this book emphasize the importance of serving your customers—but not all customers are equal. And those customers that are unprofitable can flat out put you out of business.

WHAT IT MEANS: A profitable customer is the right customer. But its important to distinguish between short term and long term profitability, and to consider the effect that working with one customer may have on other potential customers. Just ask Best Buy. In a *Wall Street Journal* cover story, Best Buy's CEO said he wants to separate the "angels" among his 1.5 million *daily* customers from the "devils." The devils are its worst customers—the ones who buy products, apply for rebates, then return the items; or who present rock-bottom price quotes from hole-in-the-wall Internet merchants, demanding Best Buy make good on its lowest-price promise; and so on and so on ... ad nauseam.

Best Buy believes that up to 20 percent of its customers are not profitable for them, so they want to focus on the people who buy products without waiting for markdowns or rebates. Your business has "devils" too, and you don't want to waste time with these types. They'll negotiate you to the bone. Just like they did with the supplier before you, and the one they'll try it with after you.

ACTION PLAN: Develop measures that will help identify your customer devils. Flag them in your database. And empower your sales and customer service people to politely but firmly limit or refuse service. By all means, go the extra mile and proactively delight your best customers, but your customer devils are just a drag on your staff and your profits—weed them out!

EVEN BETTER: Most managers have heard of the 80–20 rule—that 80 percent of your business comes from 20 percent of your customers. The same probably applies to your customer service problems. Periodically review your sales and service policies that may be subject to abuse and try to plug the loopholes. Establish a system that can help prevent customer devils from taking repeated advantage of you.

RULE EIGHTY-FIVE
LEAD BY EXAMPLE

Whether you like it or not, you are a role model to your employees or staff. They may not always look up to you, but they are always looking at you. If you say one thing but do another, you are sending a dissonant message that could adversely impact your image and effectiveness as a manager.

WHAT IT MEANS: What makes a business grow? Leadership. The leadership and vision of the entrepreneur light the way for business success. You and your employees follow the course you have set for the business. Be sure that you lead by example when it comes to working hard, valuing lifelong learning, and appreciating employees' contributions. Your personal attitudes and actions influence those around you.

Some people just love their chosen occupation and nothing makes them happier than doing a good job. They enjoy meeting and helping people. They're enthusiastic. These owners or managers are enthusiastic and positive around everyone—especially customers and employees. People want to be surrounded by positive people. A leader who may not be charismatic but is positive draws a positive response from those he or she interacts with. A positive outlook can help develop a can-do attitude among employees and can generate a feeling of goodwill among customers.

ACTION PLAN: Start acting immediately as the person you will be, a person of character with a sound reputation. Your words, your manner, your attitude, your dress, your posture, and your actions are all reflections. In modern society, people are constantly bombarded with visual and auditory messages. People need cues to sort good from bad and to find order so that they can make decisions. In many different aspects of your daily life, you are giving off cues that can be positive or negative. If you speak well, dress appropriately, smile, are courteous, work hard, volunteer, and don't complain, you give people shortcuts to view you in your best light.

EVEN BETTER: Identify some great leaders whom you admire, learn more about them, and then strive to emulate their leadership style.

RULE EIGHTY-SIX
WRITE FAN LETTERS

There are probably a few business leaders, speakers, or consultants (including, perhaps, the occasional business book author or two) whom you read about and whom you'd love to meet and maybe even work with. Don't let their fame—or misperceived high price tag—get in the way of your getting together.

WHAT IT MEANS: It's a small world, and people are far more accessible than you might think. Often, a good letter to said superstar is all it takes. Why a letter? Because this is the medium that is more likely to get through the gatekeepers than a phone call or a chance encounter on the golf course or in the rest room. Most letters, if they are serious and businesslike, will get read—and anything that gets read might yield a response. It's a long-shot to be sure, but what have you got to lose? Gaining a big-name business leader or training guru as a contact or partner in some new venture could open doors that you never even knew existed!

ACTION PLAN: Pick the special someone you'd like to meet or work with, and write your letter. Your letter is more likely to elicit a response if you're proposing something of mutual interest—getting together so that you can pick his or her brain is not likely to cut it, no matter how much flattery you pour on. If you have a specific proposal to discuss, spell it out. In other words, give your business icon a good reason to say yes. Perhaps an invitation to lunch or breakfast?

EVEN BETTER: Make your presentation values as stellar as the star. Have some top-drawer stationery designed and printed (if you don't have some already), and have your letter hand delivered. Flourishes such as these can help make the dynamic and dignified impression that can result in the favor of a reply.

RULE EIGHTY-SEVEN
BABY STEPS STILL MOVE YOU FORWARD

If you're calling on fifteen customers in a week, can you call on one more? If you're manufacturing 300 widgets per day, can you make 10 more? Before you leave at the end of the day, can you cross off one more thing on your to-do list?

WHAT IT MEANS: Small incremental gains can add up to huge improvements over the long run. In Pat Riley's first season as coach of the Lose Angeles Lakers, he faced a challenge: how to motivate a team that had already won a championship. He did it by evoking a call for a "one percent more" performance improvement. If everyone on the team could improve their field goal percentage by one point, if everyone could improve their rebounding or assist average by one point, and so on. Now it may be purely coincidental, but I don't think so—either way, the Lakers went on to have an even more phenomenal championship year, with several players on the team achieving career highs in numerous statistical categories.

ACTION PLAN: First, you need to establish your benchmark—what is the measurement unit of what you're doing and how much of it are you doing? And then do one more!

EVEN BETTER: Strive to be the Pat Riley of your organization (the slicked-back hair is optional). Get others to buy into the "do one more" mind-set. Coach it. When possible, facilitate it. And, of course, reward it. Any organization whose people are constantly striving to do a little bit more is an organization that is far more likely to prosper.

RULE EIGHTY-EIGHT
FACE UNPLEASANT
TASKS HEAD-ON

There is a natural tendency to put off doing the difficult or the unpleasant task—but that task is sometimes the thing you need to do most.

WHAT IT MEANS: Maybe you've heard this too—that what separates the winners from the also-rans is that the winners do what they have to do, whereas the less successful focus more on doing what they want to do. Sure, it's a lot more fun attending to those things that are more exciting or intellectually stimulating—or just about anything that doesn't send your stomach churning into a tailspin—but that's why they call it "work." Problems generally don't go away by themselves. More often than not, they tend to fester and grow. The earlier you can identify and resolve the problem—no matter how unpleasant—the sooner you won't be haunted by it. And, as with most things in life, you'll get more emotionally and psychologically resilient with practice.

ACTION PLAN: Identify two or three problems or situations that you've been putting off due to your own resistance in dealing with them. Decide on a course of action. Then make sure to cross at least one related thing-to-do off your list—today

EVEN BETTER: Become more sensitive to your own resistance to the "un-fun" parts of your job. Identifying your resistance is a good first step toward getting out of your own way, and it will help make you a much more productive and effective manager. It's been said that sometimes you have to get uncomfortable to get comfortable—and it's true!

RULE EIGHTY-NINE
MAKE SURE YOUR
TOOLBOX IS FULL

Think back to high school, when you did your homework (really!) but accidentally left it at home. When you told your teacher, I bet she said, "Well, it's not doing you much good there, is it?" Same with business.

WHAT IT MEANS: A mechanic has his toolbox. A baseball player has his bat and glove. In business, you have your own tools too—business card, brochure, calculator, contact database, cell phone, et cetera. Some of these things you probably always remember to take with you when you leave the office, but there may be a few more tools that could also come in handy. For example, most people realize that it's a good idea to have plenty of business cards available to hand out at trade shows—but it's also a good idea to have some brochures or case studies or samples on hand, just in case. Sometimes unplanned sales (or work-related) opportunities happen. By being prepared, you will be more likely to take advantage of them.

ACTION PLAN: Consider what tools you might need to get the job done when you're away from your office—marketing materials, computer files and programs, et cetera. If and when possible, carry them.

EVEN BETTER: Technological advances make it easier and more possible to access critical business data at any time from virtually anywhere. Learn more about them, and consider how these capabilities might be best utilized—not only by you, but throughout your organization. Also, listen to your "road warriors"— your salespeople. Their input regarding materials and tools to augment their efforts is worth seeking.

RULE NINETY
GET TO THE POINT

There is a well-known saying in the business world: "If you can't dazzle them with brilliance, then baffle them with B.S." Unfortunately, too many people treat this as a rule. Vague, waffling, and meandering communications in any form can only lead to confusion and misunderstanding ... which can cause costly errors, poor decisions, and worse. Eschew obfuscation—say it simply!

WHAT IT MEANS: The time that you spend beating around the bush (or trying to decipher the message of someone who's doing so) is time that could be more effectively devoted to something else. Don't try to be a spin doctor—your attempt will usually be seen for what it all too often is: a semitransparent attempt to divert blame or otherwise mask a problem that needs to be objectively explored and resolved. As a Pepsi executive once famously exclaimed to derail a rambling and long-winded presentation, "I asked you what time it was, not how to build a watch."

ACTION PLAN: Edit yourself beforehand by focusing in on the main points of your message and trimming away the flab. Here are some tips:

- Don't get bogged down in irrelevant details.
- Don't repeat comments unless the listener didn't hear you or she indicates she didn't understand. Say it once and carry on.
- If the idea isn't new to the discussion, don't say it.
- Eliminate extra words. When it comes to business communications, less is more—really!
-

EVEN BETTER: Encourage your reports to be as concise and relevant as possible in their communications with you. Avoid the temptation to paper over your mistakes or to baffle anyone with B.S. At the end of the day, it's about getting things done, not belaboring why they weren't. Exception: being cogent is no license to be insensitive to other people's feelings. It may take a bit more time to express empathy or to say something kindly, but those are the times when a few extra words can actually help make you a better communicator.

Don't Lose Site of the Horizon

Meetings, decisions, things to do—there is no shortage of demands on your time. And many of them may well have the virtue of being urgent, thus requiring your immediate attention—but you don't always want to have your nose so closely to the grindstone.

WHAT IT MEANS: As a manager and/or business owner, some of your most critical responsibilities are to think, plan, and invest long-term. Not only do you need a long-term plan to grow your business, but you have to have the vision and willingness *not* to apply a short-term measuring stick. In other words, some of your proposed projects—whether it's customized database software or an e-marketing initiative or a new strategic partnership—may take a while to pay off. It may well be that some of your plans with the longest payback period may ultimately be most beneficial for your business. Many publicly owned companies are mismanaged because of this "planning myopia"—their shareholders expect immediate and continual results—but yours shouldn't be one of them. If you truly want to guide your business toward long-term success, you have to think beyond the obvious, beyond your inbox, and beyond the current quarter.

ACTION PLAN: Devote at least two hours a week to "thinking long." Where would you like to see your business six months from now … in a year … in three years … and in five years? Be as specific as possible. What will it take for you to get there? When would those things need to get done to keep you on pace?

EVEN BETTER: Get your senior management team involved. This can often be done by arranging a strategic offsite retreat wherein you can brainstorm various scenarios, address your most critical long-term challenges, and develop a consensus as to how to best proceed. There are many well-qualified consultants who can help develop and facilitate such a program, and many first-class resorts that can provide a suitably inspiring and out-of-the-box site.

RULE NINETY-TWO
USE THE RELEASE VALVE AS NEEDED

If you're not at least a little bit frustrated by the slings and arrows of the daily grind, you're probably not working hard enough, too burned out to care, or are already emotionally intelligent enough to have made this rule part of your standard operating procedure. Everybody else—read on.

WHAT IT MEANS: Sometimes they are small, and sometimes they seem as huge and heavy as the world itself, but frustrating things happens. Deals fall through. You're passed over for that promotion you thought you had nailed. Your assistant made the wrong decision without taking the time to ask you. Your boss chewed you out in public. Sometimes you can attempt to defuse the source of your frustration by confronting the individual or reevaluating the situation (maybe Joan in Accounting really isn't out to get you). Sometimes, though, you just have to suck it up and take your emotional bruises home—but you owe it to yourself, your professional demeanor, and to others *not* to be a seething volcano of resentment. It's almost impossible to make cool, level-headed decisions when you're seeing red.

ACTION PLAN: Be aware of what's eating you—and don't let it eat you! Identify the problem. Decide whether it is feasible or worthwhile to deal with it, and how to do so in the most constructive way possible. Remember to choose your battles wisely—a jerk of a boss or colleague is not likely to change his or her ways simply because you decide to confront him or her. It's not that you should never take the chance—just realize that your results may vary.

EVEN BETTER: Strive to keep your frustrations to a manageable level by not getting all bent out of shape at every perceived slight. Accept that a certain amount of work-related frustration is par for the real world. Try to adopt a more long-range perspective: chances are that what's bugging you today won't be renting space in your head a few weeks or months down the road. Everything passes—including your foul moods.

RULE NINETY-THREE
CREATE AN "US" MENTALITY

Your effectiveness as a manager is highly contingent on the collective efforts of your team. The way you act and the things you say can help build team motivation and solidarity—or hamper it.

WHAT IT MEANS: Make sure to share the credit for all your team's achievements.

Some managers may talk a good "team program," but they don't hesitate to take all the credit for themselves when they can (that is, when no one on their team is within earshot). You probably wouldn't want to work for a manager like that—so don't be a manager like that.

It's OK to praise or rebuke people individually, but try as much as possible, through both your words and your deeds, to communicate that you are all in this together, that you value everyone's contribution and talents, and that, at the end of the day, it really is about "us."

ACTION PLAN: Take a few moments at the beginning of each team meeting to praise or critique specific team achievements. When communicating to upper management, don't hesitate to give credit to your team and to specific team members. Great managers understand that business is indeed a team endeavor, and they know how to use praise and recognition to keep team spirit high.

EVEN BETTER: Go beyond praise to build solidarity and reward team achievements with a celebration lunch, dinner, or special event. Think about recognizing and rewarding outstanding achievement with your own (team-voted?) player-of-the-month award. Let your team know in every way you can that you're proud of them—and that you're counting on them.

RULE NINETY-FOUR
SEE THE BIG PICTURE

It's important to "sweat the details," and the successful outcome of many projects, plans, and presentations depends on it, but good managers need to have sharp long-range vision too. Sometimes fixing the immediate problem ignores the fact that said problem is just a symptom of an even larger problem. Try to see a little further.

WHAT IT MEANS: Like a car, businesses are complex integrated systems, and you can't just focus on one system to the exclusion of others. What's good for Marketing may not always be good for Production—especially if Marketing forgot to tell Production about the anticipated spike in demand expected to result from their new promotion. This isn't just about keeping everyone in the loop. It's about considering how various plans and problems impact all the areas of the business. It's about considering long-term solutions over quick, easy, but temporary Band-Aid fixes. And it's about thinking two or three moves ahead of your competition even as you're thinking about your current move. It's the kind of thinking that can lead to more critically considered decisions—and that's just a smarter way to manage.

ACTION PLAN: Before committing to a decision, give it a 360-degree view. How is it likely to impact on other areas of your business (and what can be done to minimize or avoid negative impact)? Does it mesh with your strategic long-range plan—or might you be inadvertently steering your company in a new direction? What can/should you do to sell the plan to your boss or garner the support of other managers or your team? What new problems or issues might it create?

EVEN BETTER: Challenge your team members to view their ideas—and yours—from a big-picture perspective. You can coach this by asking them questions that force such critical evaluation—and demand that this approach be followed independently in the future.

CREATIVITY LEADS TO SUCCESS

Creativity is certainly one of the essential skills that belong in every good manager's toolbox. This doesn't mean you have to paint like Picasso or sing like an *American Idol* finalist. The fact is that we all have a deep reservoir of creativity within us that is there for the tapping. Some of us are just better at tapping into it—but it's a learnable skill that's well worth developing. In addition to the bottom-line benefits your creative thinking can bring to your business, there is just something quite exhilarating and fulfilling about being able to hatch a new idea and implement it.

WHAT IT MEANS: Think about it—every successful new product or, for that matter, new business once began as a glimmer of an idea in someone's mind. Every problem that can't be solved by relying exclusively on your experience or a "sensible" approach requires at least a dash of creativity. Great ad campaigns, cool product and service innovations, making the most of your limited resources—none of that happens without some sparkling creativity. Now, it's true that some strokes of creativity are more bold and breakthrough than others, but virtually any business can benefit from a more imaginative, flexible, and intuitive consideration of its challenge. Of course, not every creative brainstorm is going to yield a brilliant rainbow, but the process can yield some very intriguing results. See for yourself—think different!

ACTION PLAN: Take a seminar or read a book that will help you develop your creative potential. Just as you can move about in different ways—by walking, hopping, skipping, or jogging, for example—so are there different styles of thought. To let your creative self flourish, you have to learn how to switch off your inner critic and set some of your cherished assumptions (presumptions?) aside.

EVEN BETTER: Give yourself and your staff permission to be a little bit out of the box and off the wall when trying to generate new ideas and/or solutions. Get a little silly. Have a little fun. Sometimes creativity begins where "normalcy" ends. Also, stimulate your mind more by exposing it more to music, art, and fresh air. Sometimes a long walk in the park or around town can spark new ideas even when you're not consciously trying to think about work.

Be an Armchair Psychologist

As a prerequisite for attracting more customers and providing superior customer service, you need to get into your customers' heads. That's the kind of information that isn't fully revealed by marketing databases or by tracking buying preferences and patterns—which is why you need to dig a little deeper.

WHAT IT MEANS: The more you can understand why your customers are buying from you—and what key factors influenced their buying decision—the more you can leverage this information into more on-the-money marketing, advertising, and strategic planning decisions. People buy things for all different kinds of reasons—price, proximity, availability, to fill stated or unstated needs, because you placed a coupon in the weekly shoppers' periodical. Those reasons may not always be what you think they are—and they are just too important to guess—so make it your business to learn what really makes your customers your customers. Once you gain this information, you can incorporate it into your marketing materials, and thus make your message more appealing to like-minded prospects.

ACTION PLAN: Encourage both formal and informal research as a means of determining what your customers' "hot buttons" are. You can do a survey (reward participation with a small gift or an entry into a sweepstakes drawing), encourage your sales reps to ask their customers and compile this anecdotal information, or conduct focus groups with customers and noncustomers. You can test customer reaction to new products, new ad messages, or your overall business image.

EVEN BETTER: It also can be useful to discover why prospective customers don't buy—as this can reveal the obstacles, psychological and otherwise, that your advertising people and/or salespeople may need to address.

RULE NINETY-SEVEN
NEW GETS OLD FAST

To everything there is a season—and that includes new product ideas and consumer tastes. Even the hottest products don't last forever. Enjoy riding the wave while you can—and do whatever you can to sustain it—but don't rest on your laurels.

WHAT IT MEANS: Best sellers can drive your business to a whole new level—but nothing lasts forever, and in our global, Internet-aided economy, your competition is more likely than ever to catch on to your stroke of brilliance and knock it off (within legal limits) as quickly as you can say "Taiwan." The solution: always be innovative. Don't just sit around waiting for lightning to strike—plant a field of lightning rods. As Charles Kettering, a very successful inventor, once said, "The best way to predict the future is to invent it."

ACTION PLAN: Don't leave it just to yourself to be your company's idea person. Try to harness everyone's creativity via a suggestions program or periodic innovation-brainstorming sessions. Sometimes, it's just a matter of creative packaging. Let's say you've solved a problem in a particularly original way for a client. You could then present it as an effective solution to other clients or prospects who might be facing the same problem.

EVEN BETTER: Realize that innovations don't have to be quantum-leap breakthroughs to be successful. Little tweaks can do the job too. Witness the iPod: different colors, different models, loads of cool accessories—you get the idea.

ONE BROKEN LINK CAN RUIN THE CHAIN

Remember that school-teacher-strict English lady on that TV quiz show a few years ago? Each round, she would tersely dismiss the poorest contestant with her withering catchphrase, "You are the weakest link—goodbye!" It's a smart way to manage your business too.

WHAT IT MEANS: Like rocks in a stream or a leaky gasket in your car, it doesn't take much to impede the smooth functioning or potential success of your organization. It could be a toxic employee or manager, a problem department, or perhaps a process or policy that's tripping you up—whatever it is, it needs to be identified and fixed—fast! You can certainly make an attempt to intervene and correct, but if the problem persists, it's probably time to get a new link.

ACTION PLAN: Look for bottleneck areas in your business. What's slowing it down? What people just aren't pulling their weight or seem to be a continual source of static and drama? Don't avoid the possibility that you might (however unintentionally) be part of the problem. Keep your ear to the grapevine, and listen to what your coworkers and customers are saying. Where there's smoke, there's usually fire—but don't wait till you're badly burned to respond to it.

EVEN BETTER: Set clear, measurable guidelines and standards so that people know what's expected of them. Also, try to have backup or contingency systems in place to handle overflow situations—perhaps another shift to handle peak manufacturing or shipping periods, or perhaps some arrangements with local temp agencies or external service providers to get you over the hump as needed.

RULE NINETY-NINE
LEARN THE JANITOR'S NAME

There are a whole bunch of people working below the radar in your workplace or as a part of your workday. The janitor. The UPS or FedEx guy. The woman who takes your order at Starbucks. The cleaning-crew lady who empties your wastebasket—and whom you see only when you're pulling a late-nighter.

WHAT IT MEANS: All of those people have names, and learning and using them, along with a greeting and a smile, might mean more than you think—and not just to them. Most people seldom acknowledge these "shadow workers," so simply by doing so, you're probably making a positive impression. Besides, you don't have to know someone all that well to add him or her to your personal network. Everybody has his or her own circle of friends, family, and associates, and you never know where it could lead. Maybe it could help you sell your car or your basketball tickets or lead to an interesting conversation ... or maybe not. Nevertheless, when it comes to extending your network, there's no need to be snobbish. Everyone counts! Being outgoing and inclusive in this way probably will seem awkward and weird at first, but you'll get used to it—and it's a very positive and attractive trait to develop.

ACTION PLAN: Introduce yourself to a few people in your company (or whom you come across in your workday). Try to greet them by name—and with a smile—whenever you see them.

EVEN BETTER: Recognition is good, but appreciation is even better. If you can offer someone a genuine compliment for a job well done, offer it. If it's appropriate to give a holiday-season gift or tip to someone, consider giving it. No matter how you do it, enabling someone to feel more valued, appreciated, or connected is its own reward.

EXPLANATIONS DON'T NEED A WORD COUNT

Can the B.S.! You may be tempted to think that a forty-page report is twice as good as a twenty-page report, but that's simply not true. Quality and quantity are two different things—and guess which one is king?

WHAT IT MEANS: Shakespeare got it exactly right: "Brevity is the soul of wit." Too many words can actually obscure what you're trying to say. Maybe in school you had to pad that term paper to some preassigned length—but school's out. In the business world, it's clarity and cogency that count.

ACTION PLAN: Mark Twain once wrote to a friend that he didn't have time to write a short letter, so he went ahead and wrote a long one. You should give yourself the time to streamline your documents with some prudent editing. First drafts have a tendency to be disjointed and rambling—but first drafts are not for the general public. Put on your editor's hat and fine-tune your document or presentation until it's crisp and right on the money. If you lack the necessary editorial skills, find someone who can work with you.

EVEN BETTER: Brevity is a worthy objective for virtually all your written and spoken business communications. When you ramble or keep repeating the same thing, you project a certain lack of confidence and professionalism. Stay on point by carefully considering what needs to be said and then saying it. You don't have to carry both ends of the conversation. And you'll get more comfortable being "short-winded" with practice.

RULE ONE HUNDRED ONE
Don't Expect Miracles

Every business can benefit from a lucky break or two, but you can't manage by wishful thinking. If you remove your rose-colored glasses, what you see is usually what you get.

WHAT IT MEANS: As the late Brooklyn Dodger general manager Branch Rickey used to say, "Luck is the residue of design." Once in a while, your business may unexpectedly benefit by being in the right place at the right time, but more often than not, you have to do your homework, allocate your resources, and do whatever else is necessary to plan for success. You can't plan for miracles and you sure can't expect them. Such wishful thinking is the very antithesis of reality-based management.

ACTION PLAN: In any situation, try not to let your desire for an insanely successful outcome cloud your good judgment. Get the facts. Don't buy into your own hype. Make reasonable assumptions and projections. You are not going to sell a kajillion of anything just because it's the coolest little gizmo you ever saw or because your Uncle Ernie said you would.

EVEN BETTER: Give your project a plan, a budget, and a time frame to succeed, with interim goals that must be met along the way. If at the end of the trial run you're not close to being there, you may be better off pursuing other goals. Trying to chase blockbusters and miracles that just aren't there can get very expensive—and hazardous for your career.

RULE ONE HUNDRED TWO
AS WALLETS GROW, SO DO NEEDS

When things are going well and your corporate coffers are flush with cash, you may be tempted to purchase things that you really don't need. The image that comes to mind is a picture I once saw of an out-of-business dot-com, its many recently purchased computers and Aeron chairs neatly stacked, awaiting a bankruptcy auction.

WHAT IT MEANS: It's one thing to reward the high achievers and dedicated managers who helped you post record results for the past quarter, but don't go overboard. Another way to phrase this rule: it's easier to spend money than to make money. Once you're basking in the glow of prosperity (temporary as it may be), all kinds of ways and means of spending money will inevitably present themselves. Some of them may even be worthwhile. Your responsibility as a manager or entrepreneur is to husband the company's capital as if it were your own—and possibly even more prudently! Your flush status may be a precious opportunity for you to pursue projects that can continue to keep your growth on the fast track. Use it accordingly.

ACTION PLAN: Develop your budget and modify it judiciously when necessary, but strive to stick to it. Delay impulse purchases by allowing a three-day "wait state" as a buffer for such impulses to cool off. Favor those expenditures that invest in the future of your business rather than those that titillate your ego. Don't let a windfall compromise your fiscal responsibility.

EVEN BETTER: Consider saving such windfalls for a rainy day—or for a highly promising new project not yet discovered. Having some discretionary money in the bank is an advantage that few growing businesses have, and it can make you a much more attractive candidate to bankers and prospective investors.

RULE ONE HUNDRED THREE
Don't Make the Boss Look Bad

This rule could very well be the most obvious one in this book. After all, what reason could it possibly serve to "dis" the boss? It's nothing that anyone with any sense would do intentionally—but there's the rub. Many otherwise sensible people show up or otherwise undercut the boss unintentionally. And at the end of the day, whether you meant to or not doesn't really matter.

WHAT IT MEANS: Don't do or say anything that might tarnish your boss's image or create a negative impression. That doesn't just mean being overtly disrespectful. It means badmouthing him or her to others, taking credit for something that he or she did, cutting him or her off in a meeting, or doing an "end around" to undercut his or her authority. All of these inappropriate behaviors could jeopardize your working relationship—and your job.

ACTION PLAN: Sometimes you may be completely unaware that you're making the boss look bad, so do a quick reality check. Through your words, attitude, tone, and/or actions, are you doing anything that would be cause for resentment? As a rule of thumb, don't do or say anything behind your boss's back that you wouldn't do or say in front of him or her.

EVEN BETTER: Consider how you can make your boss look good— by giving credit where credit is due, by keeping him or her in the loop, by seeking his or her counsel, and by generally being courteous and respectful in his or her presence.

NEVER EXPECT ONE CUSTOMER TO CARRY YOU

Many businesses begin with a single customer—say when a consultant or graphics designer starts out on her own and her previous employer becomes her first client. Nothing wrong with that—but it does leave your business in an inherently insecure position. The fix? Get more customers as soon as possible!

WHAT IT MEANS: Financial advisers advise you to diversify your investments to minimize risk. You should also diversify your business for the same reason: to reduce risk by avoiding dependency. To ensure that you remain in business, be certain that no one customer is in a position to control your company. You may lose control if you allow your business to be held hostage by a powerful customer. And it can happen easily. The only permanent thing in life is change—and that certainly includes your customers, or customer. What if your customer fails? What if another company buys your customer? What if the customer decides to buy from your competitor? Many things are possible, so dependency on one or two customers is dangerous to your survival.

ACTION PLAN: Plan from Day One to attract more customers by treating your marketing plan as fundamental to the success of your business—because it is! Advertise, cold call, use direct mail and e-mail, ask for referrals, or work with an ad agency to create a campaign that will generate a steady stream of qualified leads—but do what you can to avoid being dependent on any one customer. You just can't build a stable foundation on a single post.

EVEN BETTER: The quickest way to get from one customer to more customers is to develop a basic marketing plan and implement it. If marketing is not your core competency, read some books, take a class, and talk to friends or associates with more experience in this area. You don't have to do everything by yourself, but you do owe it to yourself to get up to speed; that is, to the point where you understand what your marketing people (or ad agency) are doing and why. Don't pass the buck on this one—acquiring new customers will always be the lifeblood of your business.

RULE ONE HUNDRED FIVE
PROTECT AND SERVE YOUR BRAND

A brand is essentially how people perceive your company, your products, and even you. It's the basic overall perception that your customers and prospects have. Obviously, having a positive brand image can be a strong competitive advantage. People may often do business with you based solely on their perception of your brand, so it behooves you to manage those impressions for maximum sparkle and shine.

WHAT IT MEANS: It takes more than slick advertising to build a strong brand. You have to back up your claims with strong performance. Are your products reliable or, better yet, exceptional? Is your service a customer turn-on or turnoff? Every single impression that your customer has of doing business with you counts—what she hears from others; what she experiences herself; and what you communicate via your marketing materials, your logo, your packaging, your product design, the appearance of your store or reception area, et cetera. Ideally, all these factors should work in sync to proclaim the glory of your story—but all it takes is one bad apple, one discordant note, or one scratch on the new car to ruin the effect.

ACTION PLAN: Regularly probe for factors that might be tarnishing your brand. Can product/service quality and/or value be improved? Does your advertising speak to the reasons people are actually buying your products? Are there weak links in the chain—products or packaging or people who reflect poorly on your overall brand? Do your corporate communications (including ads and Web site) have a similar look and feel to reflect consistency and solidity? Like goodwill, your brand is an intangible asset—but that doesn't mean that it can't be managed.

EVEN BETTER: Do some research to gain a more accurate sense of how your brand is perceived. Your preconceived notions may simply be wishful thinking, so make sure to ask the people who really know: your customers and prospects.

RULE ONE HUNDRED SIX
Sing Your Own Praises

If you're in marketing or advertising, this rule has undoubtedly already been tattooed onto your brain. For everyone else: you need to give people credible and compelling reasons to buy what you're selling. And that means you have to think in terms of what's in it for them.

WHAT IT MEANS: Every ad, brochure, e-mail, or direct mail is an opportunity to win customers and drive sales—but people don't buy things to keep you in business, they buy what they think they need. Your challenge is to discover those needs and address them. To the extent that you can identify problems and position your products or services as solutions, your marketing messages will be more effective. Many business owners are so enamored with their offerings that they focus—to their disadvantage—on features.

For example, having an ergonomically designed shovel handle is a feature that provides the benefits of being able to work more comfortably and for a longer period without hand fatigue. Having the shovel zinc-plated means that it will never rust, which could mean that it's the last shovel that you'll ever have to buy. Let your benefits drive your ads, and your ads will drive more customers through your doors.

ACTION PLAN: Review all your ads and marketing materials. Are the benefits clearly stated? Could they be stated with more zing? Also, keep in mind that not all benefits have equal weight. Focus on the two or three main benefits for clarity and impact. You can include the others, but giving your readers too much information (at least when trying to spark initial interest) can dampen interest. You might very well have nine or ten great reasons to buy your product—but your prospects' eyes are likely to glaze over before they get that far. Also, read a book on copywriting to gain a better sense of how the pros do it.

EVEN BETTER: Look for hidden product benefits—those that might never occur to you—by surveying or talking with customers. You can incorporate these newly found benefits into future ads, and you may even come away with some valuable and quotable customer testimonials!

RULE ONE HUNDRED SEVEN
Improve Customer Service

You know how important customer service excellence is to the success of your business. It will help attract more customers and keep them coming back. It will generate more word-of-mouth referrals and positive impressions. Indeed, exceptional service is such a rarity these days, that achieving it—or even aiming for it—is almost certain to establish a significant competitive advantage. Nevertheless, this is one area where "good enough" isn't. You need to aim high—and keep trying.

WHAT IT MEANS: Organizations exceed customer expectations by focusing their improvement efforts in three areas: customer-friendly processes, employee commitment to customer service, and customer dialog. You must be excellent in all three areas to achieve excellent customer service. This is one area that needs to be micromanaged or extensively scrutinized and evaluated. A customer service seminar or retreat session for your workers or managers is a good start; a customer service suggestion or rewards program is a good idea—but it takes more than this to create a corporate culture that's truly committed to service excellence. Everyone, from the top down, has to walk the talk. Processes have to be made more customer-friendly. Continual customer service improvement is possible, but it must be continually pursued.

ACTION PLAN: There are five pillars that can help you get from good to great: find and retain quality people, make service a core value (so employees can think beyond the policy manual), empower frontline employees with the discretion to make customers more satisfied, solicit and use customer feedback, and pick the right customers (decide who your core customers are, and do what you can to woo and wow them).

EVEN BETTER: Try doing business with your company. Place an order, call tech support, request some sales literature, or try to get a return authorization— or have some "service-quality scouts" do this for you and report back to you. The results could be very enlightening. The more you can view every facet of your company from your customers' perspective, the more clues you'll gain regarding potential areas of improvement.

RULE ONE HUNDRED EIGHT
BE ENTREPRENEURIAL

This is the age of the free agent. Even if you're not the owner of the company you work for, act as if you are. Seniority and experience simply don't have the value they once did. You have to do more than just show up and put in long hours. You have to produce profits—and results.

WHAT IT MEANS: Entrepreneurship is the recognition and pursuit of opportunity without regard to the resources you currently control, with confidence that you can succeed, with the flexibility to change course as necessary, and with the will to rebound from setbacks. It means being resourceful—using what you have to do what you can.

It means taking the initiative—making the success of your business your ultimate responsibility. And it means that you bring to the table a certain amount of passion and "sweat equity"—the willingness and energy to roll up your sleeves and tackle the many problems at hand. Clock-watchers need not apply. Regular employees have jobs. As an entrepreneurial person, you can have a mission.

ACTION PLAN: Be creative in acquiring the resources you need to build and grow your business—or your career. Learn what you need to know. Establish goals and work toward them. Be a "company of one." Don't hesitate to take educated risks. First and foremost, an entrepreneur is a person who takes responsibility for making things happen, including his or her own job satisfaction. Plain and simple: your success is ultimately up to you.

EVEN BETTER: If the business where you currently work is too small for two (or more) entrepreneurs, do what thousands of underutilized, underappreciated, and underfulfilled people have done before you: start your own business! Take a course, read a book, do the footwork, and start planning a venture that will make you "boss-free" from Day One.

RULE ONE HUNDRED NINE
Convert Energy into Results

Sometimes in a meeting, or perhaps a more private discussion, a truly intriguing idea will be advanced. Your ears perk up. The room is electrified. You can almost cut the "Wow factor" with a knife. That doesn't necessarily mean that the idea will pan out, but you can and should use this motivational "peak moment" to your advantage.

WHAT IT MEANS: Plain and simple: make the excitement work for you. With the momentum of enthusiasm on your side, it's like running downhill. You will surely cover more ground in less time—so don't wait for the glow to fade. Turn the inspiration into action by getting everyone involved in specific tasks that can either explore the feasibility of the idea or actually make it happen.

ACTION PLAN: Decide then and there what needs to be done to put the idea into play. Have an impromptu strategy session to develop the project framework—things to be done, who will do them, and when. Make it clear that you're excited by this Big Idea too, by your willingness to fast-track and support it.

EVEN BETTER: Realize that any idea, no matter how brilliant on paper—especially those ideas that upset the status quo—is almost bound to be met with a certain amount of resistance. Part of your responsibility is to garner a groundswell of internal support—in other words, to sell it. Consider effective ways to do this as part of your overall plan. Who will you need to talk to? What will you need to say?

RULE ONE HUNDRED TEN
FIND YOUR YODA

A good mentoring relationship allows both mentor and mentee to develop new talents and build self-awareness. In business settings, the mentee can become more in tune with a corporate culture, and the mentor can hone leadership skills. But arguably the toughest part of a mentoring relationship is finding a mentor. Don't expect results overnight, but do what you can to cultivate potential mentor relationships.

WHAT IT MEANS: Having a mentor (or a few—there's no rule that says you can have only one) is one of the smartest things you can do to advance your career. He or she can be an invaluable ally, supporter, and guide—someone whose wise perspective can help you more adroitly navigate the treacherous shoals of office politics; someone who will take a genuine and ongoing interest in watching your back and helping you advance to the next level. Who wouldn't want that? That being said, mentors are not fairy godmothers—you don't get one just for being the main character in your own story. You need to make a conscientious effort to identify appropriate mentors and make yourself an attractive mentee. First and foremost, there has to be good personal chemistry—do you and your potential mentor really and truly click? Would-be mentors are most receptive to people who ask good questions, listen well to the responses, and demonstrate that they are hungry for advice and counsel.

ACTION PLAN: Consciously think about where you are in your career, and where you would like to be. Honestly assess what type of personality you have, and which personality types complement your style. Consider your strengths and weaknesses, and define how a mentor might guide you through your growth. If you don't know yourself, how can another person support you and help you grow? Also, try to keep an open mind regarding who this person might be: A mentor is someone who will help you grow in the area(s) most important to you. This person is not necessarily your supervisor or anyone with a high-ranking title or even someone in the same business. Look for someone who exemplifies the traits and skills that you want to adopt. If your accountant models the **mind-set management behaviors that you strive for, she could be your mentor.**

EVEN BETTER: Understand that the relationship is a two-way street. The mentor might also benefit from some of the skills, competencies, and perspectives that you bring to the table. The best working relationships are mutually beneficial. Ask not only what your mentor can do for you …

RULE ONE HUNDRED ELEVEN
IT'S A JOB, NOT A PRISON SENTENCE

There are times—perhaps more than a few—when you will feel frustrated, burned out, and downright trapped by the way things are going at work. Fortunately, most of those feelings will pass, or at least subside—but when they don't, it may be time to move on.

WHAT IT MEANS: Gone are the days of lifetime employment with one company. Downsizing, outsourcing, and the general turbulence of today's global economy have changed all that. It's the Age of the Free Agent—and it means that there is no chain trapping you to your desk. Obviously, deciding to quit your current job is not something that you should do casually or impulsively, but if your day-to-day work experience has just become flat-out miserable, with no relief in sight, you're not doing yourself any favor by staying there.

ACTION PLAN: Always have an exit strategy. Keep your resume current and your cover letter sparkling even when times are good—because you never know. Put the word out through your network that you're looking, and gear up for an active and aggressive job search. Let your dissatisfaction motivate you toward extracting yourself from your current "career prison" ASAP. After all, in the final analysis, all jobs are temporary—and when it comes to leaving a job (or boss) you despise, change is good.

EVEN BETTER: Determine whether it's possible to improve your job situation by trying to confront the problem—or whether it's possible for you to engineer your own attitude adjustment. If your pain stems from a specific situation, perhaps that situation can be resolved. If it's a whole laundry list of horrors, it's probably time for you to plan an expeditious retreat—but walk away professionally, with a smile, a handshake, and no burned bridges. In any case, don't lose sight of the fact that insofar as working at any job goes, you do have a choice.

WHAT GETS MEASURED, GETS MANAGED

If you want to make sure that certain things get done, make sure that you have some way to measure and monitor them. Simply knowing that someone is keeping score can be a powerful incentive for those involved to measure up—and for your business to stay on track.

WHAT IT MEANS: Establish baselines and determine the data requirements to reference, measure, monitor, and verify your environmental performance and progress. Choose meaningful starting points that you can use to reference your progress. These baseline indicators may be things such as number of sales calls made per week, percentage of sales calls resulting in a sale, profit per item sold, total response to a particular direct mailing, et cetera. Make sure that your metrics are meaningful. For example, it may be nice to know that your customer service reps handle about twenty calls per hour, but that may not necessarily correlate with delivering excellent service, because some complaints or queries simply take longer to resolve.

ACTION PLAN: Decide what measurements might help you more effectively gauge the operating performance and fiscal fitness of your business. Your accounting people may be able to provide good counsel in this area—but also seek input from your staff and other managers, even those outside your company. What three things would be most useful for you to measure? What systems would have to be modified and/or implemented to track it?

EVEN BETTER: Not everything worth measuring can be boiled down to a simple number—but measure it anyway! Some managers have embraced the concept of the "balanced scorecard"—a report card that specifies and weights the various performance criteria for excellence. The worker is then periodically "graded" by his or her supervisor (and, if appropriate, his or her team colleagues). Simply making those performance criteria clear and relevant to all can be a big step toward encouraging people to walk the talk—because what's measured is much more likely to get done.

KEEP YOUR GOALS WITHIN PLAIN SIGHT

It's good to have goals. It's better to write them down and give them deadlines and action steps—but to really keep your eyes on the prize, you need to stay focused on those goals, literally!

WHAT IT MEANS: The workplace is a minefield of distractions—from the relentless barrage of e-mails to the inevitable mini-crisis of the day—and sometimes, to be sure, it is all you can do to attend to the matters at hand. It's also true that your boss's priorities can, at any time, become yours. Nevertheless, if you don't keep reminding yourself about what you want to do—about your personal and professional agenda—then who will? Just as the very act of writing down your goals helps crystallize them and make them more attainable, so does being regularly reminded of them generate an ongoing awareness … which maintains motivation … which will eventually lead to actions … and results!

ACTION PLAN: Make a list of your top ten goals (personal and professional). Now post this list in places where you can't help but see it—your refrigerator or bathroom mirror, your PC or PDA, your top drawer or wallet (on the back of your business card). Believe it or not, even if you have not done a thing all day to advance toward those goals, you have done something of immense importance: you have not lost sight of them!

EVEN BETTER: Once you're regularly focused on your goals, figure out strategies and steps toward getting there. Can you do something every day to advance toward at least one of them? Can you do three things each week? Obviously, there are going to be some days when your pursuit of your goals will be detoured by the demands of the day—but with your list of goals front and center and reviewed each day, at least you'll be a runner who has the finish line in sight.

HALF-ASSED WORK LEADS TO HALF-ASSED RESULTS

Sometimes we are all tempted to coast—to give a project a perfunctory, halfhearted effort. And even though you may have the best excuses in the world for not giving something your best effort, the quality of your work tends to speak loud and clear for itself.

WHAT IT MEANS: Don't phone it in! Case in point: An elderly carpenter was ready to retire. He told his employer-contractor of his plans to leave the house-building business and live a leisurely life with his wife enjoying his extended family. He would miss the paycheck, but he needed to retire. They could get by. The contractor was sorry to see his good worker go and asked if he could build just one more house as a personal favor. The carpenter said yes, but in time it was easy to see that his heart was not in his work. He resorted to shoddy workmanship and used inferior materials. It was an unfortunate way to end a dedicated career. When the carpenter finished his work, the employer came to inspect the house. He handed the front-door key to the carpenter. "This is your house," he said. "My gift to you."

The carpenter was shocked! What a shame! If he had only known he was building his own house, he would have done it all so differently. So it is with us. We build our lives, a day at a time, often putting less than our best into the building, then with a shock we realize we have to live in the house we have built. If we could do it over, we'd do it much differently. But we cannot go back. Build wisely!

ACTION PLAN: Often, "coasting" at work is related to stress, fatigue, or a negative attitude. Don't let any of those factors prevent you from delivering your level best. Part of being professional is being consistent regardless of your feelings or physical or emotional state, so be aware when your commitment to doing a good job starts to dip. It may be better to take a break or make an attitude adjustment and get it done a little later than to do work that reflects poorly on you. If your work were a painting, would you be willing to sign it?

EVEN BETTER: Make yourself more resilient to the blahs by keeping yourself physically and mentally fit. Eat well and get the rest you need. Have a life outside of work and strive for balance. While it's only human to have an off day or two, you don't want to make a habit of it—and healthier habits are a great safeguard.

RULE ONE HUNDRED FIFTEEN
MAKE GOOD USE OF YOUR "IN BETWEEN" TIME

In the course of your day or week, you may spend a fair amount of time in traffic, in reception areas, or on line. Instead of simply cooling your heels or impatiently waiting for your turn, use these random moments for pleasure or productivity.

WHAT IT MEANS: Time is indeed our most precious resource—no matter what we do (or don't), we get only one day to use every day. The secret to getting more things done isn't necessarily to race through the day at breakneck speed, but to use our time more consciously and judiciously. There are those who might listen to audio-books on their daily commute, or tap out a quick memo on their PDAs. Others might prefer to relax to music, or to review the main points that they intend to make during their imminent meeting. One need not strive for 24/7 productivity. Nevertheless, those "dead spaces" during our days can be used more meaningfully than you might think.

A friend of mine recently told me how he just happened to pick up the local business journal while he was waiting to meet with a client. Thumbing through the pages, he noted a few ads by companies that might be good prospects for his services. He jotted down the contact info, shot out his e-marketing brochure when he got back to his office, and had a quick call-back and scheduled meeting with a potential new client by the end of the day. Now that's making great use of your in-between time!

ACTION PLAN: Be prepared. Carry some reading material, a voice notes recorder, or even some of your favorite music with you wherever you go. Consider listening to a training tape or business book during part of your commute or during your lunch break.

EVEN BETTER: Take a few moments to take stock of your personal goals. Have you done anything to advance them today ... or this week? If the answer is no, what might you do to change that?

RULE ONE HUNDRED SIXTEEN
Always Consider the Source

Whenever you hear something work-related—no matter whom you hear it from—don't take it at 100 percent face value. Most people will not flat-out lie to your face, but they can often be very "selective" in what they tell you and how they spin it.

WHAT IT MEANS: Self-interest can be a major stumbling block to objectivity, and there are few places where self-interest is more prevalent than in the workplace. People want to keep their jobs. They want you to view them in the most favorable light. And information (or the appearance of it) is power. Bottom line: people are biased, and because of this, the truth can often get bruised and bent as people tell you what they think you want to hear—or what they would like you to believe. Listen carefully and critically, but don't necessarily believe everything you hear. Some people are simply more reliable than others.

ACTION PLAN: Factor in the credibility track record of your source. Has she or he been reliable and trustworthy in the past? Is there anything about the content of his or her communication that doesn't ring true? Ask questions. Dig a little deeper to separate facts from opinions. Interpretations can and will vary, but the facts shouldn't.

EVEN BETTER: Do what journalists do—verify the accuracy of your information by checking it out with another source or two. Sometimes the story will look quite different from someone else's perspective. Also, try to be as objective and "spin-free" as possible regarding all of your work-related communications.

RULE ONE HUNDRED SEVENTEEN
START AND END MEETINGS ON TIME

If you're not the boss or meeting manager, this rule is obviously not applicable—but even if you're not, there will probably be a time or two in your career when you are tasked with running a meeting, and Rule #1 of effective meeting management is "Run meetings on time."

WHAT IT MEANS: The more people in the room, the more schedules (and overall productivity) your meeting will affect. Letting all participants know exactly how long a meeting will take is not only considerate, but it also enables people to plan accordingly and stay on their schedules. It tells them that you value their time. And it demonstrates that you're an effective manager—able to stick to your agenda ... and word. Nobody appreciates meaningless meetings that ramble on endlessly—so, at the very least, by adhering to a clear agenda and timetable, you'll be doing everyone a favor.

ACTION PLAN: Start and end on time, no matter what. Don't wait for people to show up. Don't waste time with break-the-ice small talk—this is not the time for water-cooler chitchat. Make sure everyone has a copy of the agenda beforehand, and dig right in. Manage the tendency to go off topic by nipping it in the bud. Say, "That's an interesting idea, Jeff, but I think it's too far afield from this meeting's agenda. If it's OK with you, I'd like to bring it up for discussion at our next meeting."

EVEN BETTER: Manage meeting expectations. It's better to schedule an hour meeting and have it end ten minutes early than schedule a forty-five-minute meeting and have it end ten minutes late. Also, there are times when you might consider breaking this rule; for example, when there's a great idea that you want to brainstorm further in the heat of the moment—but do so with caution. Attendance at that point should be made optional, or let there be a five-minute break.

RULE ONE HUNDRED EIGHTEEN
Do Your Homework

Whether you're making a sales call, going on a job interview, or preparing a report, there is no substitute for being as well prepared as possible—and no good excuse not to be!

WHAT IT MEANS: Doing your homework—getting up to speed with the facts, skills, and presentation materials you need to sparkle and shine—will make you far more likely to sparkle and shine. You need to take full responsibility for owning every aspect of this endeavor—after all, it's your career. If your research skills aren't sharp, either sharpen them or enlist a sharp delegate who can help. Gather evidence that will build your case.

Statistics and results always speak louder than opinions. Decide how to best weave your selling points together into a coherent and compelling flow. Learn as much as you can about the process beforehand. For example, if you're getting a performance review, request a copy of the evaluation form prior to the review, so that you'll be in a better position to anticipate and discuss each criterion. In general, the better prepared you are, the more confident, polished, and successful you'll be.

ACTION PLAN: Do your "homework" regularly, by reading up on your industry and gathering data to support your ideas and projects even before you are formally charged with developing and/or presenting them. Explore what online sources might be available to support your case. Envision what it would take to be perfectly prepared for the task at hand, and then do the necessary homework—including practice—to get an A+.

EVEN BETTER: You don't have to bury your audience with proof, but more is usually better than less. If you already have an article or case study that clearly supports your position (or claim), don't stop there. Find another one. Let the weight of evidence (other articles, market research, internal and/or industry data, etc.) support your presentation with a resounding thud!

Don't Wait for Everything to Be "Exactly Right"

Because we live in a less-than-ideal world and usually fall well short of being omniscient, it is usually not feasible or realistic to wait until all the facts are in before making a decision or launching a new venture or project. Perhaps Napoleon Hill, America's original positive-thinking guru, said it best: "Do not wait; the time will never be 'just right.' Start where you stand, and work with whatever tools you may have at your command, and better tools will be found as you go along."

WHAT IT MEANS: Last month, a friend of mine left his full-time job to pursue his eBay sports memorabilia business full-time—something he had been thinking (and agonizing) about for several years. What made him do it now? I wondered. "Because I finally realized that it was now or never," my friend replied. "There was never going to be a guarantee of success—nor was there much chance of me being able to do everything right. Sooner or later, it just comes down to taking a deep breath and doing it. You can plan until the cows come home, but until you actually do it, it's just a dream." My friend had come to realize what many successful managers already know: you usually don't have all the right tools or information or perfect plan to do what needs to be done. The challenge is to get things done anyway—maybe that's why it's called managing. Don't get bogged down by the idea of perfection. It doesn't exist. Take action now.

ACTION PLAN: Think about two or three places in your business life where you're waiting for things to be "just right" before you take action. Consider what can be done to make progress in those areas. It is always reasonable to consider the risks of any endeavor and strive to minimize them, but "paralysis by overanalysis" can delay or prevent you from implementing the changes your business needs to grow—and that's also risky.

EVEN BETTER: Don't be a perfectionist! As a manager and a human being, you will rarely if ever have all the resources you need (including information) to make easy, foolproof decisions. There is a difference between making well informed and fully informed decisions—and the latter can be a lot more unrealistic and unnecessary than you might think.

RULE ONE HUNDRED TWENTY
LEARN HOW TO GET
PAST THE GATEKEEPER

Whether you're pitching yourself in an interview or your service or product in a sales presentation, you need to be speaking to the person who can say yes. That person will inevitably have someone guarding her door and phone line. Your mission, if you choose to be successful, is to circumvent that gatekeeper.

WHAT IT MEANS: Getting past the gatekeeper is what separates the sales superstars from the rest of the pack. It takes resourcefulness, it takes persistence, and it takes a willingness to try different tactics. What works at one company may not work at another; indeed, what worked on Monday may not work on Thursday! First and foremost, you need to do the research to determine exactly whom you need to talk to at the specific company you're targeting. Then you need to get through his or her gate.

ACTION PLAN: Here are some tips for getting past the gatekeeper:

When you call the office, treat the gatekeeper with the same respect that you would treat the potential partner. This will make them warm up to you. Sound important but courteous, for example, "Hello there, please put me through to Joe Smith."

If you happen to know someone who knows your key decision maker, ask for permission to use his or her name. When the gatekeeper asks what your call is regarding, you can say, "His good friend Norm First asked me to call him."

Adopt the gatekeeper. In other words, develop a relationship with him or her. Do this by engaging in a conversation whenever you call. Developing a relationship with the gatekeeper comes in handy when you've been unable to reach your potential partner because he or she is often out of the office.

Send a letter first. In the letter, ask the potential partner to expect your call on a certain date. This way, you can say, "He's expecting my call" when the gatekeeper asks what your call is regarding. Another approach is to e-mail your potential partner to check if he or she has received your letter, and then ask for the best time to call him or her. In this instance, it's likely that your potential partner will let their gatekeeper know that your phone call is expected.

If voice mail is the gatekeeper, it's best to send in a letter first, and then follow up by leaving a voice mail message. However, if you choose not to send a letter first, then simply introduce yourself and the purpose of your call. Keep it brief, but try to pique your listener's interest. What can you say that would make him or her curious enough to return your call or e-mail you?

EVEN BETTER: Go where—or when—the gatekeeper ain't! Call executives during off-hours—between 7:30 and 8:30 in the morning and after 5:00 in the evening. Trade shows are also a good place to gain "face time" with senior managers with less restricted access.

RULE ONE HUNDRED TWENTY-ONE
GET CREDIT BEFORE YOU NEED IT

It's only a matter of time before your business will need money. Perhaps you will need to cover operating costs during a temporary slump. Perhaps you are bursting at the seams from a rapid growth spurt. Or perhaps you have decided to invest in a new computer network or expand your manufacturing capability. New and not always predictable reasons for needing to borrow cash will inevitably occur—but smart owners and managers should not wait till the last minute to explore financing options.

WHAT IT MEANS: Finding capital to build and grow the business is one of the biggest challenges facing small-business owners. Limited access to capital in the first two years of a business's life cycle is a major problem facing many new businesses. In addition, underestimating the need for capital and failing to understand the importance of getting access to capital are two of the most common mistakes made by new business owners. The savvy businessperson knows that securing capital is necessary to build and grow the business, and also knows that good credit makes securing capital easier. Establishing solid business credit takes time and effort, and it's important to start early in the game.

Before you proceed, make sure you have a strong business plan because it may well be required and reviewed in future lending situations. Also, understand the four Cs of credit evaluation: Capacity, your ability to repay the loan; Collateral, your assets that can be used to secure a loan, such as a building, equipment, or bank accounts; Conditions, your intentions for the loan and the external variables such as economic factors that can impact how the money lent will be used and repaid; and Character, your personal attributes, traits, abilities, and integrity, along with your education level and work experience.

ACTION PLAN: Maintain a good relationship with your bank and with your banker. You should periodically review your fiscal condition and anticipated borrowing needs with him or her. Open a business credit-card account. It's a quick and easy way to start building your business credit history. Finally, make sure to have "industrial strength" accounting systems in place—the kind that can easily help you track your sales and expenses and produce the kinds of reports that lenders want to see. Partnering with a local accounting firm could be very helpful in this regard.

EVEN BETTER: Consider other potential sources for credit if needed. These could include a loan from friends or relatives, microloans from the SBA or other private organizations, a line of credit, or better credit terms from your current suppliers. If you're about to launch a business of your own, you might want to obtain a home equity line of credit (or expand your current one), as your currently employed status will work to your advantage.

RULE ONE HUNDRED TWENTY-TWO
DELEGATE WORK, DON'T ABANDON IT

You must develop the ability to delegate the right task to the right person in the right way. It's almost impossible to grow your business without it—because there's only so much time in a day and you can increase your workload only so much.

WHAT IT MEANS: When you're encumbered with daily business issues, you're prevented from attending to the larger issues—business vision, customer relations, recruiting new talent, growth. Especially in smaller businesses, that can be a critical error. Daily stuff has to be done—somebody has to sign the checks—but if you're doing that when you should be developing your next product or service, you're limiting your future growth. That said, delegation is not abdication. You're still responsible for the ultimate results of the delegated tasks, and you must stay on top of them.

ACTION PLAN: Start by identifying the best person for the job (realizing that attitude and willingness to take on new challenges may count more than experience). Next, clearly and logically identify the goal of the project or task as well as the key steps involved. Third, establish clear milestones and deadlines. Finally, be sure to provide frequent feedback.

EVEN BETTER: After the project has been completed, review the process with your delegatee. Taking this extra step allows all the people involved in the task to identify what they would repeat, modify, or change the next time around. It also lets you determine what was learned, how well the person handled the challenge, and how comfortable/competent that person might be at taking on additional responsibilities.

RULE ONE HUNDRED TWENTY-THREE
STRIVE TO BE DIFFERENT

Customers and employees alike have certain base expectations about your business—that you'll be open during your posted business hours, that your roof won't leak, that their paychecks will clear, et cetera. Meeting these expectations may not always be easy, but they only get you to par. To really stand out from and above your competition, you have to be delightfully different—memorably distinctive in small (or not so small) ways that enable customers or employees to sincerely say, "Wow, no other company has ever done that for me before!"

WHAT IT MEANS: The first hotel to put a mint or chocolate on its guests' pillows was on to something. The one-thousand-and-first hotel wasn't. In other words, once a "delightfully different" service or employee perk gets emulated by everyone, it is no longer so different. That doesn't mean that you have to be absolutely unique to be delightful—it's all about style and providing that precious "pampered VIP" feeling. For example, some companies offer weekly massages, and I seriously doubt that any of your employees would complain if you did likewise. The goal is to try to do something enjoyable and wonderfully unexpected to demonstrate how much you value these two groups that are so critical to your company's well-being. You don't have to reinvent the wheel, but creative little flourishes add to the wow.

ACTION PLAN: Find out what other companies are doing and up the ante. Chocolate on the pillow may be a hotel industry cliché, but what if it's a handmade gourmet chocolate? Free coffee is ubiquitous—but free cappuccino or free muffins and bagels on Fridays are not. It's easy to add your own delightful twist—and it doesn't have to be a budget breaker. For example, I know of one company that provides its employees with hot or cold towels to refresh themselves. Can you imagine refreshing yourself with a cold towel after a "hot" stressful meeting? Delightful!

EVEN BETTER: Mix it up. Even the most posh of perks can get old after a while, so keep thinking of little ways to wow workers and customers. Invite suggestions. Do some "market research" to see which of several possible perks would be most appreciated. *P.S.:* There's no **RULE** that says a perk has to happen regularly or even be announced beforehand. You could order dinner in for those working late to complete an important project … or spontaneously treat everyone in the company to ice cream …or give away tickets to a local sports event in a random drawing.

Have fun!

RULE ONE HUNDRED TWENTY-FOUR
GET IT IN WRITING

In the immortal words of Ronald Reagan, "Trust, but verify" (referring to arms control with the old Soviet Union). That is, it is fine to expect the best, but you must plan for the worst. It is all well and good to do business on a handshake, but the savvy business professional knows that more is needed. The less left to misinterpretation, misunderstanding, differing perspectives, and unexpected contingencies, the better.

WHAT IT MEANS: First of all, it means that no matter how well you know your business associates, no matter how much you all trust one another, you have to get all important agreements in writing. The fact is, memories fade over time, people remember things differently, and people choose to remember things differently, so the only way to avoid misunderstandings is to record any and all agreements in writing. If you're an independent contractor, don't begin any job until you have written authorization. Doing so is smart business and no one should be surprised or offended if you insist that your agreement be in writing after all, it protects the other side as much as it protects you.

A few years ago, a friend of mine started a business that looked like a goldmine almost from Day One. She soon brought in a few partners (and their money) and business continued to grow. So far, so good … until it wasn't. Sales hit a brick wall, tempers flared, and soon the partners' investments were all at considerable risk. It became a legal and emotional ordeal, and although it all eventually ended well, the experience was a hard but valuable lesson for my friend—namely, that even the best of business plans and the friendliest partnerships can tank. And on that sad day, you'll be a little less miserable if you remember to follow this rule. Lawyers notwithstanding, promises, words, and handshakes are simply not as binding as written contracts.

ACTION PLAN: Make sure to routinely use contracts and purchase orders to back up your company's promises to perform or to secure the goods and/or services of others. Write down your employee policies—and make sure that they are communicated and understood. Unless you're a lawyer, don't write your own contracts. Either use a real lawyer or get templates of frequently used business agreements from the Net or one of **your business associates.**

EVEN BETTER: Having a signed contract is one thing; knowing where to find it is another. Make sure that all of your contracts, including invoices and purchase orders, are easily accessible. For extra security, keep backup copies of your most critical contracts at a remote location.

RULE ONE HUNDRED TWENTY FIVE
KEEP THE DIALOGUE GOING

Make it your policy to respond to all e-mails and telephone calls as soon as you can. Reply quickly even if you don't have an answer or new information to report. It's always smart to let those who try to reach you know that they and their problems are important to you. Explain that you're working on their matter and that you will get back to them as soon as you have something concrete to report. If you can, estimate how long you think it will take to get them the necessary information.

WHAT IT MEANS: Although people want results, they also want and need attention. They want to know that they are not being ignored, especially when they're paying or doing business with you. When you acknowledge and promptly respond to their inquiries, most people will be reasonable and more patient. However, if you fail or take forever to answer, they will be more likely to become incensed, demanding, and more difficult to work with.

ACTION PLAN: Set aside a specific time each day to answer e-mails and phone calls. Your response can be brief, even as little as an acknowledgment of their attempt to reach you. Try to respond the same day you were contacted. Consider prompt responses a part of the service package and professionalism that you provide.

EVEN BETTER: If you're away or can't reply, instruct someone to respond promptly on your behalf. Tell him or her to explain that you're tied up and that you will get back to the caller or sender at the earliest opportunity. Have him or her ask if there is anything that he or she can do while you are unavailable.

RULE ONE HUNDRED TWENTY-SIX
TRUST YOUR INSTINCTS

When you make decisions, listen to that little voice inside you. It knows what it's talking about! Examine all the alternatives, take your time, but don't dismiss your first reactions unless major doubts persist that convince you that you were wrong. Be true to yourself and don't discard deeply held feelings simply because others don't understand.

WHAT IT MEANS: Often, when we react quickly, strongly, and can't immediately explain our reasoning, we second-guess ourselves and question the validity of our initial feelings. We may be afraid that we acted too quickly, impulsively, emotionally, or without sufficient reasons. Trust yourself; your instincts are not just whims or brainless, superficial responses that just popped out of your head. They are the products of your accumulated knowledge, experience, feelings, and wisdom. The fact that we can't readily explain them should not invalidate them. Experience has shown that our instincts are usually right.

ACTION PLAN: When you instinctively react, let time intervene. Try not to think about, belabor, or implement your decision. Time has a mysterious way of providing the right answers and removing unnecessary doubt. Let your initial reactions sink in, and live with them before making those decisions final. Then, if you still have nagging doubts or others convince you to the contrary, you still can change your mind.

EVEN BETTER: Don't reveal your instinctive reactions. Instead, say that you need additional time. Then, let your reactions percolate and subject them to the test of time. If they continue to feel right, implement them. If not, try something else.

REWARD THOSE WHO DESERVE IT BEFORE THEY ASK

Never get into the position in which an employee asks you for a promotion or a raise. Instead, always stay on top of your employees' performances and reward them before they ask for more. Beat them to the punch. Giving unsolicited promotions and raises delivers the message that you appreciate the employees and value their efforts on your behalf.

WHAT IT MEANS: Whenever an employee asks for a promotion or raise, a problem exists. (1) If the employee deserves the boost, you should have been more observant and properly shown your appreciation for the employee's efforts. Failing to reward top people is a great way to lose them. (2) If the worker doesn't deserve a raise, he or she has unrealistic expectations, which you—as a good boss—should have realized and addressed. In business, money is generally considered the way everyone keeps score!

ACTION PLAN: Communicate closely with your employees, check their performance, and create an open atmosphere in which you interact. Make them feel free to come to you for guidance and help. However, don't let workers become dependent on you for answers they should know or find out for themselves.

EVEN BETTER: Create performance incentives. Set production levels and give rewards for surpassing them. Be clear on the targets they must reach both in terms of the amount of work to be produced and the quality at which it's completed. Production can greatly increase when employees have a stake in the game.

RULE ONE HUNDRED TWENTY-EIGHT
DON'T GO TO MEETINGS EMPTY-HANDED

Prior to attending a meeting, even if it's with just one other person, set the agenda; know exactly what you want to accomplish at the meeting. Decide beforehand on the topic you plan to discuss, how you will introduce it, and precisely how to proceed. Anticipate who might disagree with you or try to divert you and how thwarting you would benefit them.

WHAT IT MEANS: Whoever controls the agenda can exert the greatest influence on the direction the meetings take and the results that can be achieved. That person has the best chance of controlling timetables, deadlines, and the personnel assigned to implement all tasks. He or she can also control or influence the finances. Succeeding in business often depends on gaining and maintaining control.

ACTION PLAN: Plan ahead. Identify the ultimate outcome you hope to achieve and lay out each step required to reach your goal. Learn about the people you will be meeting with, how they work, and how various outcomes would impact them. Arm yourself with the heavy artillery: reports, studies, surveys, and other documentation that will support your approach, quash opposition, or convince them to join forces with you.

EVEN BETTER: Beat potential opponents to the punch. Quickly, neutralize them or convert them to your position by understanding their views, showing them the strength of your reasoning, and/or offering them incentives if they work with you. Find out what they want and see if you can offer them more or see that they get it sooner. Understand their skills and talents and how they could be utilized for your benefit.

OFFER BETTER ALTERNATIVES

Don't criticize unless you can suggest better alternatives or approaches. Most people have some personal investment in the positions they put forth and may take exception when others shoot down their ideas without offering better suggestions. If, however, you explain how alternatives could be more advantageous, others may accept your reasoning and not take it personally.

WHAT IT MEANS: If you repeatedly find fault but don't suggest better approaches, people will ultimately stop listening to you. You will be viewed as negative, disruptive, and not achievement or team oriented. You will be avoided and could fall out of the loop. It's easy to be critical, but offering viable alternatives takes work; it forces you to think, learn, and examine better ways, not just react.

ACTION PLAN: Always try to find out what is going to be discussed and think it thoroughly through in advance. If something is suddenly sprung on you that does not feel right, don't immediately dismiss it. Explain that you need more time to think about it before you commit. Then, examine it more deeply and search for better ways.

EVEN BETTER: When presented with weak ideas, it may be beneficial to help those who suggested them to come up with better solutions. When you determine that they're off course, don't knock their conclusions. Instead, offer suggestions that you could explore together. Present just part of the picture or point them in the right direction. Then, let them find better answers. When people play a role in solving problems, it can give them more of an incentive to see that their plan succeeds. And, it can encourage them to think matters through more completely in the future.

SMALLER PORTIONS NOW CAN LEAD TO BIG DIVIDENDS LATER

Whenever you have to split an uneven amount of money, always take the smaller amount. For example, if you have $99 to divide, give the other person $50 and keep $49. It's not the amount that matters—even a dollar will make your point. The small amount you give away is a tiny price to pay for goodwill, and that goodwill can last for years. In fact, when dividing almost anything, take the smallest portion if there is one.

WHAT IT MEANS: When you voluntarily take the lesser amount, it shows that you're not cheap, petty, or small-minded. It's also a sign that that you're generous. Small acts of generosity can help you become a more generous and giving person. They can also make you feel good! People respond to and like to spend time with those who are generous; usually, giving people are not as tight and are more pleasant. If you get a reputation for generosity, people will want to deal with and spend time with you.

ACTION PLAN: In your financial (and other) transactions, consciously look for opportunities to give more than your share. Don't go overboard, but make small, generous gestures when you're splitting tabs and other expenses. Never point out that you took less or paid more than your rightful share. If others comment, accept their thanks graciously and pass it off casually as if it were not a big deal.

EVEN BETTER: Periodically, pick up small tabs, especially when it's for people who are not on your financial level. Think of it as a way of saying "thank you" or showing your appreciation. Again, don't brag, grandstand, go overboard, or try to buy someone's favor. Do it to be generous and to say thanks.

FIND PEOPLE WHO KNOW MORE THAN YOU DO

You can't do everything yourself and do it all well. It's simply impossible. Everyone needs help with something or other. So, find experts who excel at what you don't do particularly well or at tasks that are not an efficient use of your time. Seek people who are at the top of their fields and have a consistent track record of accomplishing exactly what you need. Don't just get help, get expert help; hire the best you can find.

WHAT IT MEANS: Hiring the best can be expensive, but often it's well worth the price because experts bring so much to the table. First, they usually know the answers or where to go to find them; they're not learning on your dime. Experts usually have extensive experience and know the ins, outs, and all the shortcuts, which will save you time, aggravation, and money; they know how to avoid red tape. Plus, experts have contacts with other outstanding people, who can help you expedite matters, avoid potential problems, and bring you greater success.

ACTION PLAN: Network. Contact the most successful people you know and learn who they use. Ask them to tell you about the expert and what they like and don't like about him or her. Ask your contacts to introduce you, or get permission to use their names. Verify all recommendations with people in your network, visit each candidate's Web site, and Google them. Read everything you find and prepare a list of questions to ask when you contact them.

EVEN BETTER: Interview all candidates personally, face-to-face. Ask them specific questions regarding how they would handle some of your actual problems. Whenever possible, visit their place of business to get a fuller sense of who they are and how they operate.

RULE ONE HUNDRED THIRTY-TWO
LEAD WITH PASSION

Empires may start with great, innovative ideas, but their success is usually fueled by their leaders' passion. Ideas are plentiful, and when standing alone, they're seldom enough. To be successful, they must be well implemented and strategically directed. Passion energizes ideas; it creates the excitement that drives their realization and success. Business leaders' enthusiasm attracts supporters, followers who believe in their leaders' visions and will tirelessly strive to make them work. Supporters who feed off their leaders' passion will enlist others to advance the cause.

WHAT IT MEANS: All successful businesses need direction; they must continually be kept on tract. They must have a mission and be true to it. Great leaders excel at providing that direction. They succeed because they are convinced of the value of their mission and excel at communicating the depth of their belief to others. Great leaders' passion inspires and excites others and convinces them to follow their lead.

ACTION PLAN: Unleash your emotions so that they come across in your actions and speech. Express your true feelings, but don't exaggerate or become overly dramatic. Always be honest. Excitement is contagious when it's genuine, but people can sense if what they're told doesn't ring true. If they don't believe you, they will turn you off and you can end up **preaching to an unreceptive flock.**

EVEN BETTER: Surround yourself with advisors who are objective and will tell you the truth. Then, listen to them. Passion can be a double-edged sword. Although it can excite and inspire others, it can also keep you from seeing or not giving sufficient weight to flaws in your basic thesis or approach. Have your advisors constantly monitor you to make sure that you don't stray.

YOU WILL GET AGGRAVATED—PLAN ON IT

In making decisions, many people overlook signs that indicate that their choices could be the source of major aggravation down the road. Aggravation can be a killer: it can sabotage schedules, block initiatives, monopolize valuable time, and prevent you from making the best judgments. Before making important decisions, consider the aggravation factor. Specifically ask yourself which of your options is most likely to give you a real headache?

WHAT IT MEANS: Aggravation produces stress, and like a virus, it can insidiously seep into all aspects of your life. It can disrupt your business and spill over into your personal life. As a result, it can alienate you from bystanders who innocently drift into your line of fire. Aggravation, and the stress it may cause, can dim your focus and drive you into making decisions for the wrong reasons.

ACTION PLAN: Train yourself to identify situations that have the potential to trigger subsequent trouble. Make it a standard part of your decision-making process. Trust your instincts; if you get the slightest inkling that an aggravating situation might arise, stop and evaluate the matter in greater depth. Analyze it in terms of the worst-case scenario by asking what is the greatest damage that could occur and estimating how much it could cost you. Then, if you still wish to proceed, you will have identified the risks you could face.

EVEN BETTER: Chose the less aggravating alternative, even when it's more expensive. Eliminating such annoyances can add years to your life! Balance the additional amount you would have to pay to avoid aggravation against the liability you might incur under the worst-case-scenario analysis. Exposing yourself to aggravation in order to save money can be a costly gamble.

RULE ONE HUNDRED THIRTY-FOUR
ACKNOWLEDGE ALL CORRESPONDENCE

Whenever someone sends you mail or e-mail, other than mass mailings, promptly acknowledge it. At the least, thank them for the message. A quick acknowledgment is a courtesy that tells them that you read their message and want to remain in contact. It will buy you additional time to get back to them with any substantive information they may have requested.

WHAT IT MEANS: Businesses are based on building strong, productive relationships. Building these relationships is a cumulative process that takes time and effort. A key factor in forging good and lasting relationships is creating goodwill. Those who promptly respond and acknowledge contacts create goodwill because they don't leave others hanging. People want to work and do business with individuals who are responsive and with whom they have built goodwill.

ACTION PLAN: Quickly reply to correspondence regardless of how small or insignificant it is. When it clearly calls for a response, get back to the sender as soon as you can. If you can't provide what the sender requested, state that you will get the information to him or her shortly. When correspondence is sent to you only to keep in touch, still promptly respond. Often, these communiqués are thinly veiled feelers, and your reply—even if it's just to decline for the moment—will keep the channels of communication open and help build goodwill.

EVEN BETTER: In addition to mail and e-mail, acknowledge phone calls. Usually, simply sending a brief e-mail is all you need. People will appreciate the courtesy, which will strengthen your relationship.

RULE ONE HUNDRED THIRTY-FIVE
Keep Everyone Up to Date

When a number of people are involved in a project, their success often turns on how well they coordinate and work together. While they are working on projects, team members may get immersed in their specific tasks and their parts can take on lives of their own. As a result, they may lose sight of the team or other team members, drift, fall out of step, or get lost.

WHAT IT MEANS: When working with others, operate as a team. To do so, each team member must understand his or her role in and know how his or her performance impacts all other team members as well as the project as a whole. Any action by one or more team members can change the project to some degree. So, if others are not informed about changes or developments in the project, they can end up operating in the dark, in a vacuum, or on an alternate plan that could move the project in the wrong direction.

ACTION PLAN: Keep everyone on the team informed so that everyone stays in the loop. Make all decisions or give instructions by sending e-mail to the person or persons affected and copying all other team members. When you issue face-to-face instructions, immediately confirm them by e-mail and copy the rest of the team. Prompt e-mails will let any team member quickly dissent, make alternate suggestions, or request further discussions, which could help the team avoid costly mistakes.

EVEN BETTER: Designate one team member to notify the others of changes. As soon as a decision is made, inform that member so he or she can immediately e-mail the information to all other members of the team.

NEVER LET YOUR
RESUME GO OUT OF DATE

Periodically update your resume so you can promptly send a version that contains your most current information. When people request your resume, they usually want it relatively quickly; they generally don't want to wait until you get around to sending it. If it takes forever to arrive, the delay could damage their opinion of you; it might even take you out of the running. When they are forced to wait, requesters' enthusiasm about you or the project may wane. So, put yourself in a position to strike while they're still fired up.

WHAT IT MEANS: It's impressive to promptly receive a strong, up-to-date resume. It indicates that the candidate is attentive, responsible, well organized, and professional. Periodically updating your resume will give you the opportunity to review your career, assess your current status, and see what you need to reach your goals. It may also jog your memory about old ideas, projects, or directions that you may now be in a better position to tackle or revive.

ACTION PLAN: Review and update your resume at least every three or four months. Enter it on your calendar as a task for you to complete. Keep a copy of your most current version in your desk and in between updates, attach information that you may want to add, such as notes, clippings, business cards, photographs, and articles. They can serve as helpful reminders when it's time to update again.

EVEN BETTER: Customize your resume for each request; don't send the same information in response to every request. Shape each customized version to emphasize how your experience and accomplishments will be valuable to each of those making a request.

RULE ONE HUNDRED THIRTY-SEVEN
NEVER SETTLE

People frequently have the option of accepting what they're given or trying to get something more or better. Leaders tend to want more, but the great, visionary leaders always demand the best. These outstanding leaders require the best from themselves and they insist on surrounding themselves with others who are and want the best; nothing less will satisfy them.

WHAT IT MEANS: Those who stand pat usually prefer safety, and as a result, they may collect fewer rewards. Leaders want rewards, not safety. They want to play the game and win. They love the action, to spend their time with experts, top people, kindred spirits who have complementary knowledge, know-how, tastes, and ambitions. They want to be with those who generate the most exciting ideas, stimulation, and opportunities; those who can take them to the loftiest heights.

ACTION PLAN: Surround yourself with the best and the brightest. Few things can enhance your life and be more beneficial than spending time with those who are smarter and wiser than you. They can lift you to their level and beyond. Find out who they are, learn about them, discover where they meet, and try to get to know them. Read everything they've written, each speech they've given, and all articles and information available on them. Hire them, send them business referrals, work them into your business and your life.

EVEN BETTER: Become the best. The surest route to meeting the best is to become the best at what you do. Top people want to be together, so they tend to congregate. Become the best and you'll be invited to join the club.

Know the Xs and Os of a Phone Call Before You Make It

Prior to making telephone calls that will involve major, complex, or compound issues, write a list of all the items you would like to cover. During telephone conversations, it's easy for the parties' focus to be interrupted or diverted and for important issues to be overlooked or inadequately addressed. Preparing a list that you can follow as an agenda will make your phone calls more productive.

WHAT IT MEANS: Since e-mail is now the preferred method of communication, telephone calling has taken on a different role. It's now reserved primarily for situations in which e-mail may not be most efficient. Frequently, phone calls are preferable for important conversations that involve negotiations or when you want to make voice contact in order to stress critical points or leave no doubt that particular information has been delivered and properly understood. Deals are often closed, problems solved, and disputes settled during telephone calls.

ACTION PLAN: Draw up your list before you call, preferably the night before. Then review it the next morning and make all necessary changes. Before placing your call, e-mail your list to the other party. Explain that these are the items you wish to discuss, so he or she can prepare. Sending your list can steer the conversation toward more efficient and productive results.

EVEN BETTER: If you e-mail prior to a call, ask the other party to address any issues that don't require discussion in an e-mail reply. Then you won't have to cover them during your telephone conversation. If agreements are reached during your call, summarize them in a confirming e-mail and promptly send it while what you agreed upon is still fresh in your minds.

RULE ONE HUNDRED THIRTY-NINE
BE SECURE, EVEN ON THE GO

It's easy to leave important items behind—they slide under beds in hotel rooms; into seats in airplanes, taxicabs, and restaurants; or onto the floor when you're working at other places of business. Getting back forgotten items can be murder—if you're lucky enough to ever see them again. Leaving stuff behind can be embarrassing or even damaging in certain situations. So thoroughly check that you have all your belongings before you walk out the door.

WHAT IT MEANS: In a mobile society, people are constantly rushing. They constantly race from place to place at breakneck speed because they're running late. Frequently, they're loaded down with enough electronic equipment, paperwork, and gear to run a military command center. Many items they tote are valuable and difficult, if not impossible, to replace. Getting them back or replacing them usually takes far more time than making sure that nothing was left.

ACTION PLAN: Form the habit of taking inventory of your valuables. Establish a system. For example, before you leave your home or office, lay out every item you plan to take and note it mentally. If you don't trust your memory, make a list or enter it in your PDA or your computer—but be sure not to leave it during your travels. Before you leave places other than your home or office, check carefully to make sure everything is accounted for.

EVEN BETTER: Count the number of valuable items you take with you. While in transit, try to recall what each item is. Then, before you leave any place you stop, check that you have the number of items you should.

The IRS Can Be Nerve-Racking; Hire People to Calm You Down

You always have a business partner—Uncle Sam. How much of your income your partner takes can be the difference between success or failure or great and mediocre profits. Killing yourself running your business and constantly taking risks makes absolutely no sense if the bulk of your profits goes to the government. To retain the maximum amount, hire a tax specialist in your field and restructure your business in accordance with the expert's advice.

WHAT IT MEANS: Our tax code is complicated; it's loaded with thousands of exemptions, deductions, credits, benefits, and special programs that have been created for who knows why. Many are industry specific, and since our tax laws frequently change, keeping up can be a challenge. Business operators who are not tax experts may rely on accountants or firms that they have used for years. Those accountants may not specialize in your particular field, so you may not be receiving all the tax benefits you could.

ACTION PLAN: Identify accountants who are the best in your niche. Ask your colleagues, vendors, suppliers, customers, or clients whom they use. Check with your attorney. Contact business schools to get the names of the top practitioners in your special field. Compile a list of candidates and interview each of them. At the interview, ask them how they would handle specific problems and what benefits they can provide that your current accountant does not. Find out what structural changes or programs they would recommend to cut your tax liability.

EVEN BETTER: Stay abreast of tax changes by subscribing to tax newsletters that cover your field. Many accounting newsletters are available online.

Have a Good Crop of Rookies on Your Team

Finding talented employees can be difficult, time consuming, and expensive. Candidates may look fabulous on paper and during interviews, but on the job, they may not fit, which can cause sticky, disruptive problems. Interns, however, can be brought in at little cost, and if they don't work out, little is lost.

WHAT IT MEANS: Student interns are a great bargain. You get bright help at minimum cost. Usually, they have great attitudes, work hard, are excited and appreciative of the opportunity, and lack the bad habits or preconceptions of many older workers. Interns can be trained in your system from the ground up. If they don't show promise, the break can be clean and painless. But if they work out, they can continue with you, even part-time as they continue with school. Interns can become gems who enhance your business for years.

ACTION PLAN: Visit local schools. Don't merely telephone; go there, make personal contact, and lay the groundwork for a continuing internship program. Meet with guidance counselors and/or the appropriate department heads. Describe your operation and explain your needs, including the precise duties an intern will perform. Ask for several recommendations. Interview all candidates at your workplace, give them a tour, and clearly detail your needs. Be wary of hiring relatives and friends' kids because they frequently want only summer jobs, and if they don't work out, it can be awkward.

EVEN BETTER: Hire older interns, especially those who are interested in changing careers. Career changers often have valuable experience that younger people lack, and they can be eager, appreciative, and enthusiastic learners.

RULE ONE HUNDRED FORTY-TWO
EVERYONE IS AN INDIVIDUAL

Business operators, especially those who started their own firms, often have tunnel vision; they see only their own needs and objectives. Frequently, they're inflexible and make unreasonable demands on their employees. They insist that their staff work with the same drive, dedication, and energy that enabled them to prosper.

WHAT IT MEANS: Everyone has different goals, ambitions, and attitudes and may not bring the same values to his or her job. Self-made businesspeople frequently believe that since they did it, everyone else can do it and should do it their way. Such thinking is simply unrealistic and creates unrealistic expectations. Workers asked to meet unrealistic demands ultimately stop trying. They tune their bosses out because they're convinced it's impossible to please them.

ACTION PLAN: Examine your expectations. Are they reasonable? Accept the fact that others aren't you. They don't have the same stake in the success of your business. They may not share your goals, ambitions, and values. What may be the centerpiece of your life, your reason for being, for them may be just a temporary stop, an experience on their journey through life. Try to understand your workers' motivation and values. Then, present your requests in a context that will conform to their goals.

EVEN BETTER: Lighten up your place of business; implement a less tyrannical management style. Socialize more with your employees; get to know them and build closer personal relations. Create situations that are not all work or business. Then build on what you learn about them to be a more considerate, understanding boss.

KEEP YOUR PEOPLE CHALLENGED AND THEY'LL KEEP YOU HAPPY

When employees repeatedly perform the same tasks over and over again and in the same old way, their performance suffers. Eventually, you will have to fire them or they will quit. Simply put, they get bored doing the same thing. Their minds wander and they make mistakes, which can be costly. As an employer, you want people who operate at peak efficiency, so your job is to see that they stay interested and focused on their work.

WHAT IT MEANS: Employees aren't machines; most of them need stimulation, and many hope to grow. Constantly repeating the same tasks, even when doing them excellently, becomes tiresome, frustrating, and feels like a dead end. Employees without anything different or stimulating to look forward to can become disgruntled and their bitterness can infect the workplace.

ACTION PLAN: Plan to meet with each of your employees, but before you do, examine what could make your employees more valuable to you and their job more valuable to them. Then come up with some reasonable alternatives that could enhance their growth and careers. The possibilities could include expanding or changing their duties, having them train others, or giving them specialized training. Investigate each option and how to smoothly implement it. Then speak with the employees. First, find out what they would like to do and directions that interest them. Then, discuss your ideas with them and see how they react.

EVEN BETTER: Give your employees ample opportunity to be creative; encourage them to find new and better ways to do their work. When they do, compliment and reward their initiative, which will promote more of the same. It will also demonstrate to them that you value their efforts.

RULE ONE HUNDRED FORTY-FOUR
THE BOSS SHOULD BROWNNOSE THE EMPLOYEES FROM TIME TO TIME

Regardless of how self-assured or in control your employees may seem, they all need to receive sincere compliments when they do well. Thanking employees for doing a good job will go a long way in letting them know that they're on the right track, and in encouraging them to continue their good work. When workers get earned praise, it also boosts their morale, job satisfaction, and productivity.

WHAT IT MEANS: Many employers, especially those who consider themselves all business or "old school," freely point out to their employees when they make mistakes, but they never give them praise for good work or for showing initiative. Employees who don't receive positive feedback come to resent it, which can cause them to decrease their efforts and sulk. Their discontent can spread throughout the workplace.

ACTION PLAN: Look for opportunities to compliment your personnel. Clearly show each staff member that you appreciate his or her efforts. Don't go overboard; be appropriate and honest. In some instances, just saying, "Nice job" will be enough. Before informing workers about their errors, give deserved compliments and explain that their work is important and how it fits into the overall plan. Then, point out what was wrong and how it can be improved. Never give false praise or compliments. Employees know when they don't deserve commendations and receiving them will diminish the impact of earned compliments you subsequently give.

EVEN BETTER: Although words of praise mean a lot, nothing says "thanks" as powerfully as tangible rewards. Express your appreciation by giving your employees gifts such as candy, flowers, tickets to events, and money. Show that your gratitude extends beyond mere words.

RULE ONE HUNDRED FORTY-FIVE
VACATIONS SHOULDN'T BE FOR WORKING

You may love your work and eagerly bound out of bed each morning looking forward to going to work. Your job may be your life, your mission, your ultimate joy, but it also can be physically and mentally destructive when you do it to excess. So periodically take time to recharge your batteries; renew your energy; and bring fresh perspectives, ideas, and input into your life.

WHAT IT MEANS: Work can be a grind; it can beat you up. It's not just the challenges and stress—the killer can be the constancy, the fact that you have to do it repeatedly, day after day, week after week, month after month. After a while, the short breaks, the weekends and holidays, are not enough, and we need more time to recharge. With constant use, even the best, most well-built machine eventually breaks down—as do mere mortals.

ACTION PLAN: Take vacations. Studies show they improve your performance at work and your health. Take nonworking vacations—working vacations are not vacations, they're work. Also, visiting family is not a rest. Get away. Hit the slopes, the beach, or the back roads. Go into woods or hide at home. Extricate yourself from your computer, telephones, and work demands. Let your body and spirit mend. Go where you can be anonymous and unknown. Let others wait on you, and relax.

EVEN BETTER: When you're on vacation, don't constantly check in, even if you stay at home. Before you leave, bring all your work up to date and arrange for others to handle emergencies if they arise. Then, don't let anyone reach you and don't return calls.

RULE ONE HUNDRED FORTY-SIX
SEND UP TRIAL BALLOONS

Prior to making important decisions, get the input of anyone who could be impacted, either directly or indirectly. When the burdens of your determinations could fall upon others—especially your employees—consult with them before implementing any changes. Solicit their opinions because they may have a deeper understanding of all that could be involved, and may be able to offer better solutions.

WHAT IT MEANS: Some decision makers mistakenly believe that they, as leaders, must act unilaterally. Although leadership involves taking command, it also requires leaders to make the most enlightened decisions, and that usually requires them to seek help. Top leaders care more about making the right decisions than they do about the images they may convey. Consulting with others before taking action is not a sign of weakness; it's an indication of strong, wise leadership.

ACTION PLAN: Enlist the help of those who may have to live with your decisions. Explain how the proposed changes would be implemented and find out how the changes could affect them. Then, specifically ask how they feel about the proposals. Forcing changes often breeds resentment and causes people to not work diligently toward success. In fact, they may take actions to prove to you that the new changes don't work. However, if you can get them on your side before the changes are made, it can help ensure their success.

EVEN BETTER: Clearly explain the reasons for the proposed changes so your needs and objectives are fully understood. When your reasoning is clear, it can clear the path for helpful suggestions. If the proposed changes could be harmful, find out what you could do to neutralize such harm.

RULE ONE HUNDRED FORTY-SEVEN
MAKE SURE THEY
KNOW YOU'RE COMING

Life can be extremely chaotic and everything is always subject to change. Even the most established, concrete plans change, despite what people promise or claim. The problem is that changes are not always communicated; wires get crossed and hugely important matters have a way of falling through the cracks. To operate at peak efficiency, always confirm your appointments the prior day because it could save you time and energy!

WHAT IT MEANS: It seems like everyone's schedule is overflowing; half the world seems to constantly be juggling more than it can possibly handle. And, to make matters worse, emergencies arise, and they usually come at the worst possible times. Change is inevitable, and with some people, it's a constant part of their lives. Often, you diligently spend endless time preparing for a meeting and it's suddenly cancelled, or worse yet, you arrive, but no one else shows up.

ACTION PLAN: The day before a meeting, event, or appointment, telephone or e-mail to confirm that it's still scheduled to proceed at the agreed upon time. E-mail is preferable because it can provide a record of where and when. Double-check—no, triple-check—all dates, times, numbers, and addresses. When you confirm, clearly state how you can be reached in the event of any subsequent change.

EVEN BETTER: If you have to fly or travel any distance to an appointment, confirm the day before you leave. Don't wait until you arrive at your destination to confirm because your meeting may have already been changed or cancelled. When you're outside the United States, confirm your return flight a day or two before you're scheduled to leave.

A Business Is Always a Work in Progress

Many dominant, highly successful companies have been undercut by upstarts that took their business by responding to changes more quickly, efficiently, and economically. Although it's essential for businesses to remain true to their missions, they must also anticipate change and position themselves to turn it to their advantage.

WHAT IT MEANS: Businesses, as well as people, often get caught up in their identities. They frequently limit themselves with deeply ingrained concepts of what they think they are. They may believe that they're the "leader," the "top innovator," or the "market maker" in X, which is fine as long as it doesn't prevent them from taking advantage of exciting opportunities in Y or Z. Businesses that remain insular and don't explore new directions can become static from listening only to their own voices. It can keep them from learning about new information, technologies, or approaches that could stimulate their workforces and propel them to higher, more lucrative levels.

ACTION PLAN: Establish a policy within your organization to continuously look for new opportunities. Make it an ongoing project, a priority, and a central part of all your employees' duties. Designate specific individuals to supervise, coordinate, and report to you on the project. Solicit your staff's input on logical directions in which you could expand your core business and then explore the viability of those ideas.

EVEN BETTER: Don't wait for opportunities; create them. Start early by looking for new trends and developments as well as events that could trigger them. Then identify those into which you could move. Search for partners that could help you enter and capitalize on exciting new areas.

RULE ONE HUNDRED FORTY-NINE
READ, READ, READ

Information is the currency for decision making. To make the most informed decisions, you need the latest and most reliable information. Determining what information is trustworthy can be daunting, and the best way is usually to read. Reading can enable you to make your own, independent decision and teach you how to sift through the facts, stay abreast, and sharpen your mind.

WHAT IT MEANS: The world is awash in information; it's dispensed by television, radio, newspapers, magazines, books, the Internet, family, friends, and loads of other sources. Everyone is constantly exposed to facts and figures that often come too fast and furiously to digest. To cut through the blizzard of information, people have become headline hunters—they scan everything for key words or sound bites, rely on them, and read no further. So what they get is superficial, less than the entire story, and frequently not enough to clear the fog.

ACTION PLAN: Make reading a regular part of your life. Set aside a designated time or times every day when you can read without interruption; when you can concentrate and immerse yourself in depth. Become an avid reader; get input from lots of different sources. Find your favorites, sources that are trustworthy, and those to avoid. Instead of just relying on headlines or just one perspective, undertake your own inquiries until you feel secure with the answers you get.

EVEN BETTER: To develop the most broad and objective perspective, read a wide variety of materials. Read for business, read for enjoyment, and read for personal growth. Expose yourself to new subjects and to opposing viewpoints and be willing to explore.

RULE ONE HUNDRED FIFTY
ALWAYS BE ON TIME

When you arrive late, you send the message that you have more important things to do, that this appointment isn't your top priority. Conveying that attitude is not only disrespectful, it's unprofessional and it can be very bad business. Furthermore, if the curtain rises before you arrive, you may not be admitted. Instead, you may be forced to stand outside while the show goes on.

WHAT IT MEANS: When you run late, it forces others to wait and they can fall behind. Your lateness can waste their time, make them impatient, and raise their blood pressure, which can cause them to be less pleasant and easy to deal with. When you are not on time, it can trigger a chain reaction that pushes back everyone's schedule and decreases the time left to accomplish your business. When you're late, those who may have been eagerly looking forward to seeing you at 3:00 P.M. may be irate at 3:20. By 3:30, they might cancel the meeting and decide not to deal with you.

ACTION PLAN: Lateness tends to be an organizational problem, so constantly review your schedule in advance so you always know exactly what you have on tap. Anticipate delays, plan for them; consider it as important as planning the substantive portion of the meeting. Since delays are inevitable in many locales, build in sufficient time. If you arrive early, have work on hand that you can attend to while you wait.

EVEN BETTER: When you're running behind, phone ahead. Apologize, explain that you're en route, and see if there are any matters you can discuss, and perhaps resolve, during this call.

RULE ONE HUNDRED FIFTY-ONE
Whenever Possible, Stay out of Court

Litigation can be expensive, time consuming, and infuriating. It can also totally disrupt your business and leave all of the parties bitter, frustrated, and resentful. When parties go through court battles, their relationships are usually irreparably ruptured. Whenever possible, avoid costly lawsuits by using alternative dispute resolution such as arbitration and mediation.

WHAT IT MEANS: In arbitration, disputes are resolved by an agreed upon number of arbitrators, usually one or three. Arbitration agreements can stipulate that experts with a wide range of special knowledge serve as arbitrators. These areas can include real estate, manufacturing, entertainment, publishing, and many others. Arbitrators' rulings are final and binding on the parties and the courts. Arbitration is less expensive than litigations and concluded much sooner. Since trained arbitrators, not lay jurors, are not involved, the amounts awarded tend to be more realistic.

ACTION PLAN: In any contracts you enter, provide for arbitration or mediation as an alternative to litigation. Specify that arbitration proceedings be held in or around the area where you work or live and according to the rules of a recognized organization such as the American Arbitration Association. If you want a quick, less expensive alternative to going to court, require arbitration. However, if you want to settle problems underlying disputes and repair damaged relationships, specify mediation.

EVEN BETTER: Although mediation can be more expensive and take longer than arbitration, it usually is cheaper and faster than going through court proceedings. According to the American Arbitration Association, over 90 percent of all matters mediated are resolved to the parties' satisfaction. So, they can resume their relationships.

RULE ONE HUNDRED FIFTY-TWO
CLEAN UP YOUR MESS

We all make mistakes, but how you deal with them can be more important than the fact that you made them. Mistakes frequently cause messes, and not dealing with those attributable to your mistakes can operate against you. If you don't clean up your mess, someone else will have to, which may antagonize them and indicate that you're not willing to finish what you started or do the hard, dirty work.

WHAT IT MEANS: Mistakes are an important part of life because of the lessons they teach. They're also a natural byproduct of trying, taking risks, and assuming leadership. A crucial lesson to be learned from mistakes is that you must take responsibility for problems your errors cause. That means following through, cleaning them up, and finishing the job. If you create problems, it's your job to fix them. If you don't, it becomes a monument, a continuing reminder of your mistake, and indicates that you either don't care or think you're above fixing it.

ACTION PLAN: As soon as you realize that you made a mistake, fix or minimize the damage. Don't make excuses, blame others, or leave it for others to clean up—do it yourself promptly and without fanfare. Tackling hard, unpleasant jobs will impress others; not dealing with them or foisting them off on others will turn them off and lower their opinion of you.

EVEN BETTER: Always have alternate options in place so you can quickly implement them if your first choices fail. At every stage of your planning, factor in the possibility that problems could arise, and build in safeguards that can save the day.

RULE ONE HUNDRED FIFTY-THREE
Give Laurels to Those Who Matter

Retaining good employees is a major problem for businesses. It often seems that as soon as new workers are trained and they get the hang of their job, they move on. Then their former employers have to start the whole hiring and training process again and hope that the replacements work out. To minimize this problem, liberally reward deserving workers—it will be cost-effective in the long run.

WHAT IT MEANS: It's hard to run a successful business that has a revolving door. Constant turnover takes valuable time and resources from the main focus of your business. And some employees may leave to work for your competitors. Not rewarding deserving workers, or not rewarding them fast enough, can be a false and foolish economy. In contrast, rewarding deserving workers can go a long way toward ensuring their continued good work and may stimulate other employees to increase their efforts. Workers who feel fairly compensated usually are more productive and create less turnover.

ACTION PLAN: Closely monitor your employees' efforts; continually chart their progress. At first, reward their efforts, not just their production or the fact that they reach certain plateaus. Start by giving incentives such as gifts, acknowledgments, and awards. Then, when appropriate, up the ante with bonuses, raises, or paid time off.

EVEN BETTER: Use rewards to cement continued relationships with clients, customers, vendors, suppliers, and other business associates. Throw in something extra, give gifts, charge a bit less, or pay a little more to say thanks for their loyalty and keep them solidly in your camp.

RULE ONE HUNDRED FIFTY-FOUR
UNDERSTAND YOUR OWN PERSPECTIVE

Your perspective, your point of view, influences your decisions. Your particular background, needs, and ambitions can be powerful, positive forces that help you reach your goals, and they can also prevent you from being objective. Achieving the right balance is often tricky. So before you finalize major decisions, ask yourself whether your conclusions were objectively based. If you feel the slightest doubt, seek objective advice.

WHAT IT MEANS: Everyone has baggage that plays a role in the decisions he or she makes; with some it plays an enormous role. Your baggage may reflect your special vision and talents; attributes that may underlie your success. However, strengths can also be weaknesses, especially when they distort or keep you from clearly seeing the entire picture. For example, your pinpoint focus may help you quickly and precisely cut to the core of some problems, but may keep you from seeing even more important collateral issues.

ACTION PLAN: When you make important decisions, understand your perspective and specifically identify all factors that might be influencing you. Surround yourself with advisors who understand your perspective; individuals who have the strength and wisdom to stand up to you and say what you may not want to hear. Run all major decisions by them and give their insights great consideration. Although you will ultimately make the final decisions, don't be rushed into acting until you've received and weighed their advice.

EVEN BETTER: If you're prone to being far too subjective, back yourself up. Institute a policy that requires important decisions to be approved before they take effect. Those decisions that need approval could be classified according to their monetary value or business impact.

RULE ONE HUNDRED FIFTY-FIVE
BE CAREFUL NOT TO GET AHEAD OF YOURSELF

Think on an epic scale, but proceed in small, well-designed, and controllable increments. Don't rush, get impatient, or become greedy. Implement plans to achieve your objectives in an orderly, systematic, and attainable manner, as if you were climbing a ladder rung by rung. Trying to bite off more than you can swallow can make you choke.

WHAT IT MEANS: Remember the old adage, "Be careful what you wish for." Although clear goals are a business necessity (they motivate and provide direction), they can also cause you to overreach. It's easy to be blinded by goals, for them to become your central, most important focus and ends in themselves. When this occurs, details, even significant steps, can be brushed aside, rushed past, or not completed adequately. In your drive to reach your goals, you may try to get too much or move before you're ready, which can be disastrous.

ACTION PLAN: Clearly identify your goals and each constituent step that will be required to accomplish them. For each step, list all the assets you will have to invest in terms of personnel, time, effort, equipment, funds, and other resources. Determine which of these items you have on hand and can devote to this project. Also find out what additional items you will need and how you can best obtain them; for example, through training your existing staff, hiring new employees, purchasing, or outsourcing. Then, map out a timetable detailing how to most efficiently proceed.

EVEN BETTER: Form strategic alliances with experts whose talents complement those you lack. Partnering with others can decrease your risks, increase your knowledge, and expand your horizons by cementing new relationships that could boost your business.

RULE ONE HUNDRED FIFTY-SIX
ADMIT WHEN YOU'RE WRONG

As soon as you discover that you've made a mistake, admit it. First, acknowledge it to yourself and then to everyone who will be affected by it. Focus on quickly and decisively fixing your errors and any damages they may cause in order to minimize them. Don't make excuses; just try to rectify your mistakes.

WHAT IT MEANS: We all slip up; it's a part of life. Leaders make mistakes because they go out on limbs to make decisions. Unfortunately, mistakes can be costly, so people often try to protect themselves by burying their crimes, covering them up, refusing to admit them or accept their consequences. In the process, they often compound the damages and make the problems harder, if not impossible, to solve.

ACTION PLAN: Make it your policy to promptly admit your mistakes, especially when it could cost you. Set an example by showing those with whom you work—your staff, clients, customers, and suppliers—that you are a trustworthy professional who will take responsibility for your actions. Business relationships are built on trust. People respect and trust those who admit their mistakes, express their sincere regrets, and act promptly to fix them. When you own up to your mistakes, others will be more likely to continue doing business with you, providing, of course, that you don't constantly mess up.

EVEN BETTER: When others make mistakes, be tolerant and understanding. More can usually be salvaged through understanding than through anger or chastisement. Instead of casting blame, clearly and calmly point out the nature of the error, its full impact, and how it can be avoided in the future.

WHAT WOULD MOM THINK?

How would your mother feel about the direction in which your career is moving? Would she approve, disapprove, or voice strong opinions? Would she be proud of what you're doing and how you're going about it? Would it be consistent with her expectations and concept of success? When you need a reality check, apply the mother test.

WHAT IT MEANS: It's true: most people want their mother's approval; it's a yardstick with which they measure their success. They want their mothers to be proud of who they are and what they've accomplished. Sadly, the pressures of jam-packed, high-stakes business careers can cause people's most prized values to warp, vanish, or stray off course. In their rush to make hard, decisive, financially sound decisions, they can speed right past core values they never imagined they would lose. They may for "business reasons" act in ways that would be unthinkable years before or in other aspects of their lives.

ACTION PLAN: Reconnect with your values by measuring your progress according to the mother test; ask yourself what your mother would think about the person you've become. When business objectives seem to be forcing you to compromise your ideals, see if the actions you're about to take are consistent with the bedrock wisdom with which you were raised and the person you want to be. Remember that the answers your mother would applaud are probably closer to who you essentially are than those that would please your boss or shareholders.

EVEN BETTER: Apply the mother test to some of the thorny business decisions you face. Balance your hard, cold ways of doing business against the homespun values that your mother stressed.

RULE ONE HUNDRED FIFTY-EIGHT
REVEAL WHAT YOU WANT TO HIDE

During negotiations, disclose information up front that you would like to hide, information that if known could harm you. For example, that you failed at a similar venture, that accusations or charges were lodged against you, or that you clashed with certain individuals. Admit these problems up front because the other party may know about them or eventually find out.

WHAT IT MEANS: Pieces of the past can be embarrassing, memories that you prefer to forget. Usually, you don't speak about them because they may indicate that you did something wrong or poorly. However, if, during negotiations, you don't divulge those problems, they could come back to haunt you. If the other party already knows, your silence could be considered less than truthful and turn into a deal breaker. If it subsequently finds out, your failure to disclose could be resented and wreck your relationship.

ACTION PLAN: Assume that the other party has done its due diligence and knows about your past. It also may be waiting for you to speak up. Beat it to the punch and spin the potential problem to your advantage. Disclose the embarrassing event in the spirit of total honesty and openness. Explain how you learned, how you gained strength from the experience, and how it will help you on this project. If necessary, briefly distinguish the situation surrounding the past event from the present circumstances and avoid making excuses or casting blame.

EVEN BETTER: Approach negotiations as if you and the other party were forming a partnership. In partnerships, truth and trust are essential and can turn rivals into strong allies who forge long, successful relationships.

RULE ONE HUNDRED FIFTY-NINE
NEVER LOSE YOUR COOL

Losing your temper and reacting harshly are always inappropriate. The sting of your anger can alienate others and inflict severe damage that may be impossible to repair. Trying to lead, motivate, or convince through fear usually backfires and is counterproductive. So control your emotions even when others make repeated or costly mistakes.

WHAT IT MEANS: Everyone can get frustrated and out of sorts, but if you lose control, it can cause great harm. No one likes to work with or for irritable tyrants, people who chew them out at the slightest provocation. Irascible people breed resentment and create tense, unhappy workplaces. They stifle initiative and creativity and dampen morale and productivity. Others avoid them and won't extend themselves for them. Even if they sincerely apologize after their outbursts, it usually can't erase the wounds their anger caused.

ACTION PLAN: Control your emotions; exercising self-control is an essential part of being professional. If you find yourself about to erupt, excuse yourself and firmly, but politely, say, "I need to take a short break, but please wait because I'll be back soon and we can talk about this then." Then leave the area without looking back or allowing yourself to be drawn back in. Collect yourself and don't return until you're composed enough to discuss the matter calmly and unemotionally. If you get upset often, consider taking anger management or sensitivity training.

EVEN BETTER: List what upsets you. Understand that your feelings may be reasonable, but the extent of your reactions is both unreasonable and harmful. Anticipate when upsetting events could occur and prepare yourself to deal with them calmly if they arise.

RULE ONE HUNDRED SIXTY
DON'T CREATE EXTRA WORK FOR OTHERS

Don't pile unnecessary, extra work on others or they will make it a point to avoid you. Encourage people to perform optimally for you by limiting your requests to only what you need.

WHAT IT MEANS: Some people are insensitive; their immediate needs are all that matter to them. When others are busy, they will bust right in and ask them to do something. Usually, they're in a frenzy and act as if the world will collapse if they don't get help. Most of their requests are minor and may not cause much strain, but sometimes they can be rather complex. Plus, once they receive help, they seldom let up. They treat those who help them as if they were their personal assistants and have them jumping through hoops. Before long, everyone hides to avoid receiving more work.

ACTION PLAN: Be conscious of the amount of work involved in any requests you make. Understand how long it will take and the extent of the effort it will entail. Never ask others to do what you can easily do yourself, and try to limit the additional load you ask them to take on. Always express both your thanks for their efforts and your regrets for causing them additional work. When you repeatedly show such sensitivity, they will willingly make extra efforts on your behalf.

EVEN BETTER: Find ways to reciprocate to those who help you. Don't wait to be asked; that might never occur. Look for opportunities and small openings that will enable you to be helpful, and then act. Your voluntary actions will be noticed and will likely bring you gratitude and deep loyalty.

RULE ONE HUNDRED SIXTY-ONE
Everyone's Time Is Worth Something

People's time—even when you pay for it—is something never to be taken lightly. So value the efforts of others. If you feel that work performed on your behalf is owed to you, don't expect much and be thankful for whatever you do get.

WHAT IT MEANS: Jobs can be performed at many levels, ranging from excellent to terrible. Usually, the level of performance reflects how workers feel about their work: whether they consider it important, challenging, stimulating, demeaning, something that any jerk could do, and so on. Since workers can usually sense the importance that you attach to their jobs, you can shape their feelings. If you feel it's important, you will invariably convey that fact, consciously or unconsciously. When workers know that you place a high value on their work, they tend to make greater efforts and take more pride in their performance.

ACTION PLAN: Clearly explain to each member of your staff and everyone you do business with how their specific duties fit into your overall operation and why they're important. Tell them how all the other pieces of the puzzle hinge on their work. Inform them of the standards they must meet and make those standards high but achievable. Encourage initiative and their input by creating a mechanism for them to submit their suggestions.

EVEN BETTER: Make it a point to always say thanks and give deserved compliments, even if you only say, "Thanks for a good job." Reward initiative, great suggestions, and outstanding accomplishments. Let them always know that you appreciate their good work.

RULE ONE HUNDRED SIXTY-TWO
LEARN THE RULES BEFORE YOU PLAY

When you do business with others, it's essential to learn the rules they follow. Find out exactly what they accept and reject and how they want things done. Then deliver it to them in the fashion they want. If you don't know the rules, you can't expect to seriously compete at any level.

WHAT IT MEANS: Every game has its rules, as does every venue, business, and individual. Think of it this way: you wouldn't gamble in Las Vegas unless you knew the rules of the game you were playing—but many businesspeople operate that way. Similarly, insisting on applying your own rules is usually counterproductive because even if you have strong leverage, it breeds resentment and usually backfires on you. Learn more than just the applicable laws; learn how others interact, the methods they use in doing business, the courtesies and protocols they follow, and what they consider signs of respect and disrespect.

ACTION PLAN: Before entering into any venture, understand whom you are dealing with and study how they acted in the past. Don't simply focus on the results they achieved, but learn exactly how they proceeded to attain those results. Speak directly to people who worked with them to identify the approaches they took, how they behaved, what they demanded, what they conceded, and what they finally agreed upon. Understand their values and motivation. Measure their actions over a long time frame, but place added emphasis on the more recent past.

EVEN BETTER: Discover who wields the power behind the throne. Develop an understanding of their values and ambitions and how they exercise their power to influence or control those with whom you work.

RULE ONE HUNDRED SIXTY-THREE
GET BY GIVING

Life is a constant trade-off, a give and take. Everything has its price, especially when it comes to business. In exchanges with others, don't always try to be the big winner who gets the best of every deal. Create fair exchanges and understand that you usually can receive more if you give more—be it your money, time, goods, or services.

WHAT IT MEANS: Strong relationships are the bedrock on which successful businesses are built. So if you want to deal with the best, which you should, give them strong incentives to deal with you. People keep score: they measure what they receive by what they give, down to the last penny, object, or effort. When they sense that they're not receiving appropriate value, they may not deal with you. Additionally, people tend to be bargain hunters and want to believe that they are getting the best possible deal. It usually pays to give it to them!

ACTION PLAN: Place a value on items you want; know exactly what you're willing to give. Set the value according to the worth of the return to (1) you, (2) the other party, and (3) other potential bidders, and then see if you can sweeten your offer to make it more attractive. Develop a reputation for paying well, and people will line up to deal with you. If some try to take advantage of you, cross them off your list.

EVEN BETTER: Give generously and promptly. Be magnanimous and don't make others wait. Set a lofty standard that others will admire and respect. Giving generously and promptly will help you create strong, lasting impressions with the best.

IF IT EXCITES YOU,
YOU'LL PURSUE IT MORE

Stimulating activities tend to be more meaningful, pleasant, and less difficult. And, you usually do them better. Enhance the quality of your life, the level of your performance, and your chances of success by pursuing what excites you.

WHAT IT MEANS: Work can turn into drudgery especially when you're forced to repeat the same old tired tasks that you don't enjoy. When workers are not stimulated, time passes agonizingly and their workdays seem endless. Boredom sets in, and bored workers are generally less proficient, less curious, and less inventive. They also make more mistakes, need more supervision, and take less initiative. Frequently, they dislike their jobs and their dissatisfaction can impact other aspects of their lives. People who are stuck in miserable jobs for decades often become depressed and lead unhappy lives.

ACTION PLAN: Try to build your career around your interests by noting what you like to do. Identify the specific activities that occupy your free time— your interests, hobbies, what turns you on, and what you're good at. Examine how you could make money from them or some aspect of them and whether they could become your career. Then, determine what additional training, experience, equipment, materials, and facilities you might need and how you could obtain them. Create a detailed plan to fill your gaps and pursue your dreams.

EVEN BETTER: Be inventive, think out of the box. Ask what products or services could you provide that don't now exist. What existing products or services could you provide better, faster, or more cheaply? Anticipate future developments, where your interests could be heading, and see where you might fit in.

RULE ONE HUNDRED SIXTY-FIVE
Leave No Employee Behind

Organizations function more smoothly and proficiently when everyone is involved. When workers participate on teams, they usually contribute more than they do when working alone. Those who are uninvolved have less of a stake in the outcomes, and they usually can't step in to pinch hit when needed.

WHAT IT MEANS: Involvement makes the work more fun and the day go faster. It encourages workers to make stronger efforts. Involvement boosts morale and creates a sense of community in which everyone wants to work together for the common good. In contrast, workers who are uninvolved tend to lose interest and become bored and disconnected from projects. Then, if they're called upon to help, they frequently can't produce at the desired level. Their failures may cause additional burdens to fall on those who are already overloaded, and when they don't receive the help they need, their projects may fail.

ACTION PLAN: Stress to all personnel the team concept and the necessity of keeping everyone in the loop. Clearly explain each individual's role at each stage of all projects and designate people to serve as backups at every level. To create and maintain involvement, require workers to attend all project meetings and briefings, review all reports and communiqués, track project progress, visit worksites, and be available to assist others if needed. Create an atmosphere in which workers are encouraged to point out mistakes and to make suggestions.

EVEN BETTER: Reward initiative and helpful suggestions. Providing tangible rewards will show your appreciation and encourage workers to get more involved and make greater efforts.

RULE ONE HUNDRED SIXTY-SIX
IDENTIFY YOUR WEAKNESSES

Everybody has shortcomings, areas that are not their true strengths. Sometimes their weaknesses become Achilles' heals that do them in. To succeed in business, you must identify your weaknesses and take firm action to turn them into strengths.

WHAT IT MEANS: Although no one does everything well, some people refuse to acknowledge their flaws, even to themselves. They may be blind to their limitations or feel that any admission could be interpreted as a sign of weakness. Or they might think that such admissions might expose them to dangers that they would be unable to rebuff. Knowing your weaknesses is as important as knowing your strengths. In fact, it may be even more important because unless your deficiencies are addressed, they could become your undoing.

ACTION PLAN: Realistically identify your weaknesses so that you know where you could be most vulnerable. In your self-assessment, be ruthless: identify every area where you feel less than comfortable and could use help; don't hold back. Then, move quickly to address those problem areas before they come under attack. Usually, the best way to proceed is to find experts who excel in areas in which you feel weak. By working with such experts, you can turn your weaknesses into strengths, focus your efforts elsewhere, and save time and energy protecting your flank.

EVEN BETTER: Ask you customers, clients, and coworkers for an honest assessment of you strengths and weaknesses. Find out which areas they think could be improved and solicit their suggestions on how you should proceed. Their comments may direct or introduce you to top experts who can solve your problems.

You Are What You Produce

Regardless of the work you do, the business you're in, or the position you hold, you are your product. You will be judged by what you say, the quality of the goods and services you produce, and the manner in which you provide them.

WHAT IT MEANS: In your career, you may occupy many positions and furnish countless goods and services. During that time, many factors will change, but one constant will remain: you. The ultimate product will always be you. Over time, your clients and customers will depend on you, buy because of you, and expect you to deliver what you promise. If you do, they will continue to support you in future ventures, but if you don't, they will stop doing business with you.

ACTION PLAN: Stand fully behind your work because it will help you build a solid base of customers and clients who know that they can count on you. Only promise what you can deliver. If you're not sure that you can provide what they need or want, clearly explain the problems up front and agree to proceed only if they completely understand and agree to share the risks. Prepare for the unexpected to derail your plans. When problems strike, don't make excuses or cast blame, just fix them. Complete the project so your customers and clients always get what they expect.

EVEN BETTER: Guarantee your work. Specify in writing what each customer or client will receive, the cost, and when it will be delivered. Then always furnish it according to those terms. Guarantees will increase your business and only obligate you to provide what you should.

RULE ONE HUNDRED SIXTY-EIGHT
TURN DISASTERS INTO BONANZAS

Mistakes, accidents, and disasters are a part of business; they come with the territory. When disasters strike, act promptly to fix them; don't stonewall or give excuses. Immediately face the public or you could lose the confidence of both consumers and the financial community—and never get it back.

WHAT IT MEANS: When bottles of Tylenol were tampered with, the company immediately pulled every bottle off the shelves. As soon as the news broke, it called a press conference and announced that while only a few actual tampering cases had been detected, it was removing every bottle available in order to protect the public. Tylenol's prompt action turned a potential PR disaster into a branding bonanza and made it one of the most trusted product names in America.

ACTION PLAN: When a disaster strikes, immediately: (1) Admit that the problem occurred. (2) Apologize by stating that it should not have happened, expressing your sorrow and explaining its cause. Avoid excuses! (3) Outline the steps you've taken to ensure that it won't occur again. (4) If you don't know why it happened, explain that the cause has not been determined, but an in-depth investigation is under way. (5) Immediately investigate the disaster and how similar calamities can be prevented. (6) Detail how you're addressing the consequences of the disaster. Then, if appropriate, keep the media informed as developments occur.

EVEN BETTER: Take responsibility, even if it's not your fault. If you quickly take responsibility, the public will understand. They know that people are imperfect, that everyone makes mistakes, and that accidents happen. They will forgive mistakes but not deceit, stonewalling, and deceptive action.

RULE ONE HUNDRED SIXTY-NINE
NOTHING IS MORE
VALUABLE THAN YOUR NAME

Material objects come and go, but your name and reputation remain with you forever. Who you are is infinitely more important that what you have. The people who matter to you most will judge you more by your personal attributes than by the money you've accumulated.

WHAT IT MEANS: Everybody is trying to sell us something. And they are sending us the underlying message that wealth and possessions are the measure of success. As a result, people compete to attain material items in order to attain a more elevated status. Some of them believe that acquiring a nice home, a fancy car, and lots of expensive trimmings are all that matters, and the means they use to obtain those objects are secondary. In their drive to accumulate wealth, they disregard what others may think of them or their methods, which usually comes back to haunt them.

ACTION PLAN: Always protect your name and reputation and understand that they will take you further and last longer than material acquisitions will. When you have decisions that threaten to compromise your reputation or integrity, protect your name even though it may affect your income at that time. You can always earn more money, but you can't always repair the damage to your name.

EVEN BETTER: Most people avoid and try not to do business with those they don't completely trust. Make it your objective to be rich in friends and respect. Surround yourself with those whom you respect and who enjoy being with you because of who you are rather than the material objects you have or can offer them.

RULE ONE HUNDRED SEVENTY
It's a Marathon, Not a Sprint

When you're building a business, construct it for the long run by making decisions that will benefit you tomorrow. Always think of the future. Short-term gains, no matter how attractive, are not worth whatever you may receive if they could damage or destroy your prospects for the future.

WHAT IT MEANS: Temptation can be great. You might be asked to team up with unsavory, unethical, or dishonest characters; market questionable products; make representations that are not totally true; or do what you hate. Initially, when the money pours in, it may help you deal with your choices. However, bad decisions have a way of catching catch up with you, and they can destroy or take the pleasure out of your business or your life.

ACTION PLAN: Don't be greedy or impatient. Unless you critically need the immediate benefits to survive, pass, say "no thank you," and walk away. Don't get involved if you have even the most remote concern. Think of the long-term implications and never make any decision that could wreck your future. Consider the value of any benefits you forego as an investment in your future and peace of mind. Don't let a wrong decision undermine your future.

EVEN BETTER: Even if you need the immediate returns to survive, reject the deal. If you submit, you will be trapped and forced to continue in a bad situation. And, although people may not say so to your face, they will know and think less of you for it.

YOU WILL CHANGE, JUST MAKE SURE IT'S FOR THE BETTER

From time to time, the things that excite you will change. You may get up one morning and find that you're no longer interested in reading every little detail in the sports pages as you have virtually every day of your life. You may still love opera but no longer want to attend every performance.

WHAT IT MEANS: Face it—at age fifty, forty, and thirty-five, you're not the same as you were when you were twenty. You may feel the same, you may even look (almost) the same, but you probably have different interests. You may live in a different area, work and associate with totally different people, or be immersed in a life that varies drastically from your life of just a few years ago. In all likelihood, newer influences have stimulated you and moved you in new directions.

ACTION PLAN: Don't delude yourself into thinking that you're still the same old you or go into denial when you sense that you're not enjoying your favorite activities as much. Take it as a sign of growth and a signal to move on. Realize that everything changes and you may need new stimulation, to be exposed to something different and exciting. Don't feel guilty for abandoning or lessening your involvement with your old friends, just continue to move forward.

EVEN BETTER: Search for new challenges that excite you. They could be outgrowths or extensions of your old passions, or they could be completely new directions altogether. Either way, continue to grow. Keep yourself vital, excited, and involved by learning about and taking on new challenges.

RULE ONE HUNDRED SEVENTY-TWO
KEEP YOUR EDGES SHARP

To continually succeed in business, you must always perform better than your competitors do so that your customers and clients will feel that you're giving them great value. As soon as another business provides what you provide but does it better, faster, or cheaper, it may be too late for you to competitively respond.

WHAT IT MEANS: When some businesses do well, they become complacent. They continue doing the same work in the same way, and before long, they're no longer on the cutting edge. When these businesses are on top, they don't focus enough attention on improvement and don't investigate and/or implement new and more valuable techniques. For example, when a manufacturer grew its business, it employed the most cutting-edge production and delivery methods. However, after some years on top, it stuck with those same old methods and was undercut by newcomers who used more efficient technology that gave customers greater value.

ACTION PLAN: Don't rest on your laurels or think that you will always be the top dog in your field. Always expect serious rivals to emerge and challenge your dominance. Implement policies to avoid complacency. Continually investigate ways to improve your goods and services. Explore new directions that could enhance your existing business, provide better value to your customers and clients, and move you into new, beneficial areas.

EVEN BETTER: Make it a high priority to keep abreast of the latest developments in your industry and others like it. When you hear about new methods and techniques, contact the top authorities to learn more about them and how they could benefit your business. Then, if appropriate, get training for yourself and your staff in those areas.

DON'T JUST GET IT OFF YOUR DESK TO GET IT OFF YOUR DESK

Successful business leaders are usually great delegators. Early in their careers, they may be all hands-on, but as they rise, they learn to delegate. They master when to delegate, whom to delegate to, and how closely to monitor without micromanaging.

WHAT IT MEANS: In business, rarely can you do everything yourself and do it well. So, you must assign tasks to others and face the possibility that they won't perform according to your standards. To minimize problems, learn when to delegate or to perform tasks yourself. If you delegate, set guidelines to help you receive the level of performance you want.

ACTION PLAN: Delegate duties when you need time for more essential tasks and when you don't perform tasks well and others can complete the job satisfactorily. Don't expect others to perform as well as you, and don't be unreasonably demanding or critical. When others can perform a task well, don't refuse to delegate just to maintain control. Know both your strengths and weaknesses and those of others, and identify who could do the best job. Then, decide whether it would be more efficient for you to perform the work or to assign or contract it out. Before you delegate, list the steps required to compete the job and then set times to monitor the progress being made. Initially, monitor frequently so you can make adjustments and correct problems. If all goes well, monitor less frequently. Don't remove yourself completely from the project, but continue to play a role even if it's only to monitor.

EVEN BETTER: Retain final approval of the work you delegate. Everything you assign remains your responsibility, so having final approval should help you get the level of performance you want.

Create Career Paths for Your Employees

Everyone wants to advance and get ahead. However, in many businesses, paths upward don't exist, are unclear, or are extremely difficult or unrealistic. Help your people achieve their goals by providing avenues for them to grow.

WHAT IT MEANS: Employees perform better when they know that they will be rewarded for their efforts. They also like to think of their jobs as careers, not as dead-end jobs. The opportunity to advance is a great incentive because it enables workers to get more money, responsibility, and stature. When your people think that they have a reasonable chance of moving up in the ranks, they will usually be happier with their jobs and work harder. If they believe that their job is going nowhere, they usually won't try very hard to excel.

ACTION PLAN: Create clear, attainable paths for your employees to advance in. Write them up formally and distribute copies to all your staff. Conduct performance reviews with each of your employees at least once a year, usually on the anniversary of his or her hiring. During reviews, assess exactly where each employee stands. Precisely identify what he or she must do to reach the next level. Inquire whether the employee believes that he or she needs additional experience, equipment, or training to move up.

EVEN BETTER: When a worker is promoted, publicize it so everyone in the organization knows about his or her success. In your announcement, state how far the employee has come and in what period of time so everyone knows what can be achieved.

RULE ONE HUNDRED SEVENTY-FIVE
BLOOD IS THICKER THAN BUSINESS

Working with your family can pose unique and disturbing problems that can make both your life at work and at home difficult. When people with close, longstanding family relationships attempt to work together, it often creates disastrous results.

WHAT IT MEANS: At the least, correcting or issuing orders to close, older relatives or even to your contemporaries can be awkward. It can be the same when you're on the receiving end. Based on your close ties, family members may be prone to questioning you, and slights and disrespect may be perceived by both sides. Old rivalries and past grudges and jealousies can easily surface and affect performance. When disputes arise, family members who don't work in the business may get involved and expand the problem to a higher level. Although hiring family can be easy, firing them is not. Firing a family member can alienate you from others in the clan and create problems that may prove impossible to mend.

ACTION PLAN: Before you hire family, clearly explain to them that your business and personal relationships must be separate. Point out that you must avoid giving the impression that you are giving them favoritism and special treatment. In working with family, temper your expectations; don't expect more from them simply because they're kin. Make a conscious effort to understand, anticipate, and be sensitive to their feelings as you work with them.

EVEN BETTER: Beware of your spouse's side of the family! They aren't blood relatives, so you usually don't know them well or have a long history with them. While you may certainly place high expectations and demands on them, be aware that you simply cannot ignore family connections and the complications they bring.

TRUST YOUR COWORKERS, BUT CHECK THE FINE PRINT

Trust those with whom you work, but don't trust them blindly. When you assign tasks, trust that they will perform them properly, but also establish controls to verify that the assignment is being completed according to your requirements.

WHAT IT MEANS: Trust is the basis for building and maintaining close, productive relationships. When people feel that they are not trusted, they may initially try to earn your trust, but if it's not forthcoming, they will eventually stop trying. Ultimately, their performances will suffer and you won't get what you want. Trusting conveys confidence; it encourages people to take more initiative, be more creative, and make stronger efforts. However, in most businesses, tasks are interdependent; they require coordination, cooperation, controls, and verification.

ACTION PLAN: Find, work, and deal with only people you absolutely trust. Don't depend on anyone if you have the least question as to their trustworthiness. From the inception, fully explain exactly what you expect them to provide, the precise standards required, when their work is due, and how it will integrate with the work of others. Have them identify the benchmarks they will reach and the dates they will meet them. Explain that their progress will be reviewed at the established intervals before they proceed. Then trust them to use their own methods to perform the work and reach all plateaus.

EVEN BETTER: Establish teams to verify progress. Have those teams report regularly to you. Create a buffer between you and those who perform the specific tasks. Then oversee and work through the teams that verify the work.

RULE ONE HUNDRED SEVENTY-SEVEN
CREATE A PROBATIONARY PERIOD

When you hire new employees, establish an initial probationary period after which the individual will become a permanent employee. Explain that during the probationary period, either party can terminate the employee relationship for any reason or for no reason whatsoever. Clarify that the probation is for both parties.

WHAT IT MEANS: Hiring employees is far from an exact science. Despite how many interviews you conduct, tests you give, references you check, and other procedures you conduct, it's never certain who will work out and who will not. A new worker whom you really liked and who seemed ideal during the hiring process may be simply terrible on the job. To protect both you and the new hire, create a safety net, an escape route, that each of you can use to can get out of a potentially sticky situation.

ACTION PLAN: Set a reasonable period for the probationary term. It should extend beyond the period of training and give him or her a reasonable opportunity to show how well he or she fits in and likes and performs on the job. Although the time for probationary periods will differ from company to company, in most cases, a new employee should be able to show whether or not he or she belongs within 90 to 120 days of coming on board.

EVEN BETTER: During the week prior to the expiration of the probationary period, meet with the employee and discuss his or her performance, any and all problems, training needs, expectations, goals, and what improvements could be made. Use this conference to lay the groundwork to build a long, productive, and enjoyable relationship.

RULE ONE HUNDRED SEVENTY-EIGHT
THE RULE OF NEXT

Almost nothing in business is easy. Achieving the results you want can be a slow, tedious process. At times, you may find yourself crashing into brick walls and being repeatedly rejected, which can be discouraging and make you want to quit. If this occurs, apply the rule of next—view each setback or rejection not as a defeat, but as a victory that brings you one step closer to success.

WHAT IT MEANS: No one is born with all the answers or ability; everyone has to learn, and learning can be a slow and painful experience. When you embark on new ventures, the learning curve can seem impossibly steep. Every time you try to climb, you may fall further back, which can make you hate what you're doing, doubt yourself, and want to run. Often, in your desire to succeed, you can't see obvious problems, and you may put impossible pressures on yourself. In other words, you make your job more difficult.

ACTION PLAN: Prepare yourself for slow going; anticipate that you will probably face resistance and that it could be stiff. Accept that learning the new often takes time, especially when it's highly desirable—because if it came easy, everyone would be doing it. Remain patient and try not to burden yourself with undue pressures because they will only slow you down and impede your progress. Self-pressure will also communicate your fears and doubts to others and may keep them away.

EVEN BETTER: Find mentors, experienced people who have experienced what you're going through, have overcome the same problems, and are willing to help. Question them, learn from them, enlist them, and follow their advice.

LUNCH IS NOT FOR EATING

It often pays to conduct business outside the office, and many big deals have been made over lunch or during rounds of golf. During lunch or outings with business associates, don't lose sight of your business objectives, because if you do, the benefits of these meetings, which may have taken you forever to arrange, could go out the window.

WHAT IT MEANS: Conducting business outside of the usual business setting can be extremely productive if you keep your eye on the ball—and we don't mean the golf ball. Lunches, golf dates, and other diversions can help you and the other person relax and enjoy shared experiences that could draw you closer together.

ACTION PLAN: Mixing business and pleasure requires a delicate balance. Pushing too hard in either direction can ruin the entire experience. So can being picky about the food, service, your game, or other irritants. Before you meet, know exactly what business you want to cover and plan how to bring it up. When openings arise, use a light touch and let events evolve naturally. Make sure that you and the other person enjoy yourselves and never force discussions the other party doesn't seem to want. Keep in mind that sometimes, it may be preferable not to discuss business, but to use the occasion to set up a future meeting dedicated to business.

EVEN BETTER: If you discussed business, send an e-mail or memo listing the items discussed, confirming those agreed upon, and identifying what still needs to be settled. State how much you enjoyed yourself, express your thanks, and suggest another outing.

Some Leaders Are Born, Most Are Made

If you want to be successful, act like a leader—otherwise others won't follow you. In fact, they probably won't even listen to you. Being a leader entails more that just barking out orders; it requires you to take responsibility, provide direction, and make sure that the implementation of your plans stays on course. It means that you must learn how to convince your employees to provide you with what you want.

WHAT IT MEANS: Most workers need direction; they prefer that others take responsibility and tell them what to do. They play it safe and let others take risks. Leaders take risks, most notably by making decisions. Sure, they should get plenty of input, but the final say lies with them—as do the consequences if they're wrong. If you as a leader don't take responsibility or provide direction, others will step in or chaos will reign. In either event, if you fail to act, you will no longer be considered the leader and your chances of success will disappear.

ACTION PLAN: Study what it takes to become a great leader; immerse yourself in it. Many terrific books have been written about leaders and leadership; master them. Numerous great workshops, seminars, classes, and presentations are given on leadership training; take some and put their lessons into practice. Meet other leaders, spend time with them, and discuss mutual problems and their possible solutions.

EVEN BETTER: Find mentors. Contact outstanding people who have succeeded at what you hope to accomplish, individuals you highly respect. Cultivate relationships with them, spend time with them, and ask their advice. Learn how they think, how they operate, and the secrets of their success.

RULE ONE HUNDRED EIGHTY-ONE
EVERYONE HAS STRENGTHS— IT'S UP TO YOU TO FIND THEM

Everyone is different. People have diverse skills, interests, values, and tastes. They all have their own strengths and weaknesses. Recognize these differences and place your employees in positions where they can shine.

WHAT IT MEANS: In business, it's critical to find employees whom you can depend on, but it isn't easy because so many factors are involved. Despite the most thorough screening, an applicant you hire may not be working out. At that point, you can either (1) cut your losses by letting the employee go and starting the hiring process all over or (2) give the employee duties that will build his or her strengths and avoid his or her weaknesses.

ACTION PLAN: During the hiring process, identify applicants' strengths, weaknesses, and interests. Place the greatest emphasis on discovering the precise areas that truly interest your applicants and determine the depth of their interest. Then, try to hire those who will be working in their areas of interest, even if those areas are not their greatest strengths. When you hire them, closely monitor their progress to see if their interests are becoming their strengths. Help them along by providing them with training and chances to succeed in the areas that they enjoy.

EVEN BETTER: Develop your own talent. Find bright individuals who are eager to learn, and train them in your system. Notice the areas to which they gravitate and give them as much training as they need to master those areas.

RULE ONE HUNDRED EIGHTY-TWO
LEARN THE ART OF SMALL TALK

Everyone enjoys spending time with great conversationalists, individuals who are personable, interesting, and make them feel good. Great conversationalists rely on small talk—little, seemingly innocuous, comments and asides that keep exchanges moving and make them fun.

WHAT IT MEANS: Small talk, especially when it's injected into serious situations, helps people let down their guard and feel more comfortable—it breaks the ice. When they're more relaxed, you can get to know them and perhaps connect. Your first words or comments, which could be about the weather or last night's ball game, set the stage; they provide the opening from which everyone can proceed. As you talk, interject small talk. The livelier, more interesting your small talk, the more engaging the ensuing conversation is likely to become.

ACTION PLAN: Make yourself more interesting by reading everything: newspapers, magazines, and books. Keep current so you know and can discus a wide range of topics. Observe personable people and study what they say and how they say it. Frequently attend social and business events and seek out new people. Walk up to them, introduce yourself, and start conversations. Find out who they are, what they do, and what you may have in common. Concentrate on asking them questions and learning about them. If they inquire about you, give brief answers, throw in some humor, and then direct the conversation back to them.

EVEN BETTER: Hone your communication skills by taking acting classes, media training, or public-speaking workshops. Join Toastmasters International or the American Speakers Association.

RULE ONE HUNDRED EIGHTY-THREE
TRY SOMETHING NEW

Break the routine and get new insights, perspectives, and experiences by being adventurous and trying something new. Live dangerously, broaden your horizons, and expose yourself to different things. Being more daring could improve you, your business, and your life.

WHAT IT MEANS: It's easy to fall into patterns, to constantly repeat the same behavior and never even be aware of it. There's a certain comfort in routines; you know what's involved, you know the results you can expect, and you encounter few surprises. However, patterns can be blinders; although you steadily move forward, you may not see what else is around. You may always arrive at your destination and you probably will get there on time, but you may also miss out on so much in the world that could be enriching. Breaking molds can be stimulating, providing you with new input and helping you become a more curious, well-rounded individual.

ACTION PLAN: Begin a deliberate campaign to open yourself to the new and to make yourself more daring and experimental. Don't limit your changes to business, but make them in other areas of your life as well. Each day, do at least three things differently. For example, reverse the order in which you wash during your morning shower, take a new route to work, or eat lunch at a different time or place. Try a new brand of toothpaste, soap, or shaving cream. Instead of eating lunch alone, ask a coworker to join you. It could draw you closer and raise your relationship to a new level.

EVEN BETTER: Try something you don't like, that you never ate or always avoided. See what you may have missed, how you may have changed, or reaffirm your initial feelings.

Know Your Unique Value Proposition

Like snowflakes, no two people or businesses are exactly the same. Identify your unique value proposition, what's special about you and your business, and utilize it to distinguish you and your business from the competition.

WHAT IT MEANS: It's essential to know your strengths and weaknesses. It's taking inventory: knowing both the assets that you have available to sell and what you can't—or should not—supply. When you know your unique value proposition, you can tell potential customers and clients exactly what you can deliver. You can also zero in on the precise benefits they will get from you and why they're special and exclusive. And for which you can charge top dollar.

ACTION PLAN: Create a program to identify and continually monitor your strengths and weaknesses. Make it your crusade to continually improve your unique value proposition. Include a grading system that your staff can always see. Maintain and improve your strengths by implementing research projects, forming employee teams, and giving incentives for exceptional work and suggestions. Should your strengths fall below an acceptable level, immediately determine the reason and fix them. Also, focus on your weaknesses. If you can't turn them into assets, consider eliminating or contracting them out. In your marketing, stress your strengths and never claim to do everything better than everyone else.

EVEN BETTER: Ask your customers, clients, suppliers, and staff to evaluate your goods or services and recommend improvements. Input from customers, clients, and suppliers can make them more like your partners and give them an increased stake in your success.

RULE ONE HUNDRED EIGHTY-FIVE
ESTABLISH CREDIT

Money has a way of being available when you don't need it and becoming quite scarce when it's crucial to obtain it. Since you never know when you might need it, establish credit as soon as you can so you can get what you need when you need it.

WHAT IT MEANS: You may be in a great cash position now—your business may be operating smoothly and you're making a good buck—but who knows what your financial picture will be in the future? Things can and do change suddenly; often without warning. Your finances could get tight—you might encounter setbacks such as your invoices not being paid or arriving late or short. Or you might want to expand, buy new equipment, put on additional staff, or invest in exciting opportunities. Plus, it might be cheaper for you to borrow funds than to dip into your own.

ACTION PLAN: Plan for tomorrow today. The worst time to borrow is when you desperately need it, and the best time is when you're not so pressed. Take out a loan with an established institution that reports to credit agencies. Then, repay the loan on time or even early. This will establish a credit record for timely payments that future lenders will check. And the better your credit record, the more easily, and often cheaply, you can get loans.

EVEN BETTER: Take out a loan for a set term, say ninety days, and place the funds you receive in an interest-bearing account. On day 85, request an extension and pay the interest. At the end of the extended term, pay it off. Then repeat the process and check your credit rating.

RULE ONE HUNDRED EIGHTY-SIX
INSTALL SUGGESTION BOXES

The personnel who work in your business often have the best knowledge about the inner workings of your operation. Usually, they have the deepest understanding of how things work and how they could be improved. Often, they also have ideas that are creative, insightful, and can save your business time and money while improving productivity.

WHAT IT MEANS: Great ideas abound; they may be all around you. The people who work in your business usually have great firsthand, in-depth knowledge about the jobs they repeatedly perform. They may have thought of better, more efficient and cost-effective ways to accomplish tasks that haven't been changed in years. These old ways could be costing you dearly or preventing growth and improvements. Your workers may feel that they have no mechanism to make suggestions or they may be shy or reluctant to come forward and want to remain invisible.

ACTION PLAN: Place suggestion boxes liberally throughout your workplace. Put them in high-traffic areas where they can easily be seen and used. Also put some in places where bashful employees can feel they have some privacy or anonymity. Encourage staff participation by establishing a rewards program for suggestions that are implemented, and to ensure maximum participation, make your rewards meaningful.

EVEN BETTER: Announce the placement of suggestion boxes in a special handout that is distributed to all your employees. Also post the announcement in your newsletter, on bulletin boards, and on your company's internal Web site. Explain the details of your rewards program, and when rewards are made, identify the recipient and the amount of the reward.

Always Have an Exit Strategy

Avoid painting yourself into a corner by incorporating exit strategies in your plans. At each stage of every project, design escape routes, alternative strategies, that you can take before you get stuck in a dead end.

WHAT IT MEANS: Sometimes you get on a roll. Everything progresses so flawlessly, fluidly, and effortlessly that you get the sense that you can't fail. It's exciting and invigorating and it sweeps you up. It emboldens you and creates momentum that impels you forward toward greater gains. During these magical times, it's easy to go too far, to get careless, exceed your capabilities, and make mistakes. So, at all stages of your projects, devise alternate plans, exit strategies that can remove you from danger. Having paths of retreat also allows you to enter more boldly because you know that if you face insurmountable resistance, you can escape to fight again.

ACTION PLAN: Build alternatives into every level of your plans. As you formulate your strategy, anticipate obstacles that could arise and decide how you could deal with each. Create plans to avoid or neutralize them, but if they can't be avoided, find options that you can take. Don't sink your business by sticking with one immutable course of action. Build in safeguards, alternatives, emergency exits that will dig you out of holes.

EVEN BETTER: When it becomes apparent that your forward progress is about to be blocked, take your losses and walk away. As soon as the impasse is evident, switch gears, because wasting time, resources, and energy on the hopeless makes little sense. It's usually more worthwhile to cut your costs and move on.

RULE ONE HUNDRED EIGHTY-EIGHT
ALWAYS BE READY TO SELL

Even if you have no plans to sell your business, put it in prime condition so if you get a great offer, you can make a quick sale. Structure your business to operate at peak efficiency, which will make it more attractive to potential buyers, who might offer you a price you can't refuse.

WHAT IT MEANS: After you work for some time in a business, especially one you founded and/or built, there's a tendency to settle in, ease up, and continue doing what always worked. However, with the advent of so many new technologies and business innovations, no business can afford to stand still. In fact, they can't even move forward slowly; they must move fast. Today, new competitors are all over the horizon, and if you're not on the cutting edge, they can undercut your pricing, provide better value, and take away all your customers.

ACTION PLAN: No matter how successful your business is, you can't rest. You always must be looking to improve. Hire outside experts that specialize in your industry to assess your business. Have them scrutinize your operation, measure it against your competition, and inform you where you're stronger and weaker. Instruct them to identify new opportunities and directions in which you could expand your business and find segments of your operation that could be vulnerable to competition and industry changes.

EVEN BETTER: Consult and strengthen your relationships with your customers, clients, and suppliers. Get their input. They are frequently industry experts who create the market and can give you honest, insightful advice.

RULE ONE HUNDRED EIGHTY-NINE
ALLOCATE TIME TO FOLLOW UP

Everyone is busy ... especially businesspeople, who have a lot on their minds. And, to complicate matters, emergencies always seem to arise at the worst times. So, businesspeople may run late, not return calls, or fail to deliver as promised. To keep matters on track and to make sure that they get done, learn to consistently follow up.

WHAT IT MEANS: During meetings, you constantly hear, "I'll send it to you" or "I'll check on that." If you don't provide what you've promised, great opportunities could be lost. Following up also involves checking that others deliver what they agreed to and do so on time, and contacting those who didn't respond to you. When you follow up, it shows that you're professional because you do what you agreed and that you expect the same of others. Following up is running a tight ship, and those who do so tend to get things done—so others like to work with them.

ACTION PLAN: Every workday, devote a set period of time to following up. For example, from 10 to 11 A.M., return phone calls and correspondence and check that the items you promised others and items you expect are proceeding on schedule. Also contact those who did not get back to you. Create follow-up systems; make calendar entries and use software that will remind you. Take notes at meetings and send follow-up memos to be sure you got everything right.

EVEN BETTER: Follow up promptly. Your quick action will make it clear to others that you consider the matter to be important. A prompt, gentle reminder will usually accomplish more than harsh words, demands, or threats.

LEADERS HAVE VISION—
MAKE SURE YOURS IS CLEAR

Leaders come up with great ideas, ideas so strong that leaders are driven to achieve them. Leaders see ahead; they identify targets and their visions propel them. Even through adversity, great leaders never lose sight of their visions, and as they move forward, they have the power to enlist others to join them.

WHAT IT MEANS: It all starts with an idea: "Lets build a better ____," "What the world needs is a ____," or "I want to start my own ____." Ideas are plentiful, everyone has them, but everyone can't turn them into successful businesses. Creating a successful business takes more; it takes vision. You will know that you have vision when an idea is so compelling, so forceful, that it's all you can think of and all you want to do. It's the first thing you think of when you waken and it stays with you through the day. It energizes you, drives you investigate it fully, and you can't wait to start working on it.

ACTION PLAN: When you have a great idea, an idea that can make a difference, investigate it thoroughly. Set goals and objectives and then map out the best ways to achieve them. Inventory your resources to identify your strengths and weaknesses, what you have and what you need. Then recruit others who can supply what you lack and who have complementary talents that will help you reach your goals.

EVEN BETTER: Instill your vision in others by letting them share the rewards. When others feel that they have a stake in the outcome, your vision will become their mission and they will strive to make it succeed.

MAKE THE DIFFICULT DECISIONS, ESPECIALLY IF NO ONE ELSE WILL

Distinguish yourself by being willing to make difficult and unpopular decisions. Have the confidence and courage to decide what others would rather avoid, and to make the best decisions even though they might hurt others. Over time, individuals who consistently make sound decisions are recognized and are signaled out for rewards.

WHAT IT MEANS: Decisions can be tough; it's hard to look into the future and forecast which choice will prove to be the best. It's even more difficult to make decisions when the impact could cause other people substantial harm, especially since your decisions can make you unpopular, cast a pall over the workplace, and impact your reputation.

ACTION PLAN: Look ahead and try to anticipate the decisions you may have to make, so that you can be prepared with sound alternatives if they arise. Regardless of the pressure, don't get forced into making hasty decisions, because that's when you will make mistakes. Insist on receiving enough additional time to find the right answer. Be concerned and sympathetic about the welfare of others, and always try to reduce the pain they may suffer by trying to provide them replacements for what they might lose. Don't try to be popular; try to be fair and compassionate. If you do, people will respect you even though they may not like the impact of your decisions.

EVEN BETTER: Make the hard calls even when you may not get the credit. Consider it like making a deposit in your savings account that may not be of any immediate use but could come in very handy in the future.

RULE ONE HUNDRED NINETY-TWO
WALK UP FRONT

If you want to be a leader, you can't stand in the back. You must place yourself right up front where everyone can see you to watch what you do. You must set the tone and display the traits that you expect others to follow.

WHAT IT MEANS: Business run from top down; they reflect how their leaders operate, not what they say. When leadership is weak, business usually flounders because the employees lack direction and don't know what to do. Without strong leadership, they may make decisions that they're ill quipped to make. As the leader, you must provide direction; not just with words, but with your actions. Your employees will follow your lead and imitate you. If you don't consistently do what you say, they will do what you do, not what you proclaim.

ACTION PLAN: Take the lead, it's your drama, assume the title role. Become an inspiration for your supporting players by your dedication, preparation, and willingness to tackle whatever must be done. Set the type of example that you want them to follow. Clearly tell them what you want and explain your objectives so they know why they are so important to achieve. Dig in and don't be afraid to soil your hands. Show your staff that you are willing to do hard, unpleasant chores and will not simply pass them off to them.

EVEN BETTER: When you see members of your staff doing the dirty work, help them out. Roll up your sleeves and work with them, side by side. Take on the hardest, most undesirable chores. By pitching in, you will build camaraderie and loyalty and will inspire your troops.

Bring the Machine in for a Tune-Up Every So Often

To operate successfully, businesses need to employ the best, most capable personnel. They must assemble teams stocked with top-notch personnel who can help the business reach new heights. After you've built great teams, don't sit back and be satisfied. Continually examine how you can upgrade your teams.

WHAT IT MEANS: In business, you can't do it all yourself; you have to develop great support teams. Establish strong teams and continually examine how you can improve them. Despite how well your business and teams perform, everything can easily change. Your people can become complacent, bored, or uninspired; they may take things for granted, simply go through the motions, or become resistant to change. New methods, approaches, and technologies can overtake them and make talents that were once groundbreaking, obsolete.

ACTION PLAN: At least twice a year, conduct formal performance reviews to confirm that you have the best people handling all jobs and on all teams. Conduct informal reviews the rest of the time by keeping a sharp eye on their performances. Discuss with each employee new developments in his or her specialty areas. Have them identify new directions where the company could go and encourage them to learn more about those that could be promising. Provide the training, help, and exposure that they will need.

EVEN BETTER: Attend conferences, workshops, and seminars to meet people, feel the pulse of your industry, and spot opportunities for your company's growth. Also have your staff attend. Identify and meet the most outstanding people in your and related industries and determine if they could make strong additions to your teams.

KNOW EVERY ASPECT OF YOUR BUSINESS

To keep your business running smoothly, efficiently and profitably, learn as much as you can about every facet of it. At the least, acquire a strong overview. Even if you assign or delegate specific tasks to the most skilled experts, it's your responsibility to know how they work, what they may need, and how they're performing.

WHAT IT MEANS: You can't run a successful business in isolation. It makes no sense, and can be counterproductive, to think that you only have to know your particular niche of your business. While it's essential that you trust others to perform their duties, you must have enough knowledge about the work involved to understand when they're not performing up to speed. The ultimate responsibility for the success or failure of your business lies with you, and ignorantly relying on others to perform is a sure recipe for failure. People who understand the whole picture tend to rise more quickly to higher positions.

ACTION PLAN: Study every aspect of your business; learn how each specific area works, the problems it entails, and how each fits in with other operations. Learn what specific steps must be performed in all jobs, but don't get caught up in the intricate details involved. Observe workers in action and question them, but don't be a pest, meddle, or interfere.

EVEN BETTER: Hire a top-flight administrator or management specialist to oversee every facet of your business and have him or her report regularly to you, at least weekly. Provide a strong incentive for success by structuring his or her compensation on the results the business achieves during his or her watch.

RULE ONE HUNDRED NINETY-FIVE
Always Overstock Your Shelves

When you buy in volume, the unit cost per item is lower than when you buy single items. So, when it makes sense, save time, effort, and money by purchasing consumables in bulk.

WHAT IT MEANS: Every business buys consumables, supplies that it continually uses and replaces. These consumables can be pencils, pens, paper, notepads, ink cartridges, soap, and toilet paper, to name just a few. Businesses also need to watch the bottom line. Manufacturers and suppliers charge premiums for purchases of small amounts, but they give substantial discounts for large orders. Buying in bulk saves time and manpower. Instead of having to take time from work to purchase necessary goods, your staff can concentrate on performing their work.

ACTION PLAN: Determine when it's cost-effective to buy in bulk. Also see if you have space to store large purchases. At certain times, it may be more important for your business to have cash on hand and not to spend it on articles that you can readily buy. Measure the unit cost of bulk buys against the flexibility of having cash and factor in the time, effort, and cost you will save buying in bulk. Also add to the equation the amounts you may incur to have bulk purchases delivered.

EVEN BETTER: Lower your outlays but still get savings by forming buying co-ops with other businesses. Join three other businesses in buying office supplies in bulk and then dividing them among you. Each buying period, one of the co-op partners will be responsible for making the actual purchases.

DOUBLE-CHECK YOUR OWN MATH

Operating a business takes cash, but hopefully it also brings in cash. Ideally, it will bring in much more than it pays out. Businesses fluctuate, they go through cycles during which receivables may be slow or nonexistent and money can get tight. When your income dries up, it can force you out of business.

WHAT IT MEANS: Business is about money; it's about making money, and it's also about managing money. In business, you need money to meet your expenses and to seize opportunities that can enable you to earn more money. As they say, money makes money. So, it's essential to constantly watch your cash flow and make sure that, at the least, you have enough money on hand to meet your expenses and run your business.

ACTION PLAN: Hire a top accountant who specializes in your field and an accomplished financial planner. Work with them to anticipate your monetary needs six months, one year, and five years in advance. Create budgets and stick rigidly to them. Accumulate cash, invest it conservatively, and establish credit. Money that you don't have to immediately pay for can be better than money you have to pay now if the terms are right. Learn the tax laws and what expenses you can deduct, defer, and depreciate. Keep enough cash to cover your operating expenses for a minimum of two to three months.

EVEN BETTER: Continually review your old income and expense statements because they may give you insights on how matters fell out in the past or on trends that you may have had.

Keep Expanding Your Circle

When you attend events, don't spend all your time with the individuals you know; meet new people. Business and social events are outstanding opportunities to expand your network by making contact with new people who could become important to you.

WHAT IT MEANS: At events, it's natural to seek out friendly faces and spend most of your time talking to them. However, remember that these events are great opportunities to network and make new contacts. Follow the example of the best networkers; they move around rooms like social butterflies briefly saying hello to all their old friends while making sure that they meet new people.

ACTION PLAN: As soon as you enter a room, stop and see who's there. When you spot people you know who are with others that you have not met, approach them. Meet the new people, speak with them, and exchange business cards. Then, excuse yourself and move on. Approach strangers and continue this pattern; introduce yourself, hold brief conversations, exchange business cards, and then excuse yourself. Have a strategy to get out of any conversation, such as politely saying, "Excuse me, there's someone I have to speak with. It was great talking with you." When you see are approached by people you know, be friendly and warm, but be brief and don't let them monopolize your time.

EVEN BETTER: Try to meet the best; the speakers, the authorities, and the shakers and movers. Introduce yourself to members of the host organization's staff and ask them to introduce you to the featured speaker, head of their organization, or other luminaries you would like to meet.

RULE ONE HUNDRED NINETY-EIGHT
The Rule of Seven

According to the rule of seven, it will take you at least seven attempts before you reach your objective. So, if, after the first few tries, you haven't succeeded, don't give up, don't become discouraged—keep trying.

WHAT IT MEANS: Most good things take time; sometimes they take forever. Many people don't like to be rushed; they need time to make decisions. When they feel pressured, they may retreat and decide not to deal with you. The first time you try to solicit a new prospect or connect with an important new target, you may get through, you may even be able to make your pitch, but don't expect to close the deal. Be happy with your progress and understand that you've crossed another, important hurdle on the road toward achieving your goal.

ACTION PLAN: Formulate a strategy that includes the specific objectives you want to achieve in each of seven initial contacts. Make those goals reasonable, achievable, and not overly ambitious. Don't push too hard or ask for too much because you could scare the other party away. Move incrementally, step by step, patiently and persistently. Be prepared to make at least seven contacts before you're seriously negotiating. If, by the seventh contact, you're seriously talking, consider yourself fortunate, keep focused, and continue to work steadily to reach your goal.

EVEN BETTER: With every new approach, double your effort. During the process, don't ease up because you think you will have to go through additional contacts. Instead, try even harder, do even more to impress your targets and to consistently give them more powerful reasons to work with you.

RULE ONE HUNDRED NINETY-NINE
Everyone Wants to Sell You Something

Everyone wants to sell you something. When people say that they don't want to sell you, that's usually precisely what they're trying to do. In some form or other, we are all salespeople because we try to convince others to do or buy what will benefit us.

WHAT IT MEANS: Buying and selling is how our economy works; it's what we call commerce or trade. Buying and selling goes beyond our consumer economy; it's a part of our daily lives and is deeply ingrained in the way people interact. In many circles, sales evokes a negative connotation; it's considered unworthy, manipulative, and conniving. It conveys the idea that you're going to be taken, used, or ripped off. Ironically, the people making those judgments invariably have something to sell.

ACTION PLAN: Understand that our lives revolve around selling, around give and take and making exchanges. When people try to sell you, realize that it doesn't mean that they are trying to take advantage or get the best of you. It only means that they are pursuing what they believe will be best for them. When they start selling, don't become defensive and try to protect yourself. Instead, listen to what they say with an open mind because they could be offering you a real bargain, an item that could be of significant benefit to you.

EVEN BETTER: Monitor your own behavior. Note when you are trying to sell others. Seeing your own behavior, your own selling efforts, will make you more tolerant of others and more willing to truly listen to what they say.

RULE TWO HUNDRED
CAN THE JARGON

Every business has it's own language and terminology, which is called jargon. Using jargon within a business can be advantageous because it informs those with whom you work precisely what you mean. However, in other contexts, using jargon can create confusion and misunderstanding. It can also be pretentious and demeaning.

WHAT IT MEANS: Businesses have their own special languages, shortcuts that quickly communicate specific information in a few words or less. When insiders carry jargon outside their business, outsiders often have no idea what they mean; they're hearing a foreign language. To compound the problem, insiders often deliberately use jargon to confuse because they don't want to explain. Some insiders use jargon to intimidate, and when outsiders seem puzzled, they convey the impression that everyone understands, or should understand, exactly what they mean.

ACTION PLAN: The objective of communication is to provide understanding. In other words, you want those with whom you communicate to understand exactly what you mean. When you talk with individuals outside your business, carefully observe whether they fully comprehend everything that is being discussed. Specifically, ask them if they understood what you said and if they have any questions. If you have any doubts, ask them to explain it to you.

EVEN BETTER: Never be condescending to anyone who doesn't understand what you say. If they don't understand what you said, it's your fault for not communicating clearly, not their fault. At the first sign of confusion or lack of understanding, stop, simplify, and clarify what you want to say.

RULE TWO HUNDRED ONE
REMEMBER TO GO HOME, AND ENJOY IT

Balancing your work and family requires you to make choices, and those choices depend on your goals and values. Your goals will change with time and perhaps so will your values. The degree to which you balance work and family is an individual decision; no single answer or formula exists; it's strictly up to you.

WHAT IT MEANS: At different periods in life, we face different pressures. We also have different goals, ambitions, and resources, and our families have different needs. Sometimes all your energy must go into your career, so you can't focus as much on your family. Unfortunately, if you don't attend to your family, problems can arise. Bountiful gardens don't grow untended and neither do healthy families.

ACTION PLAN: Continually watch how you allot your time. Make sure that you're not shortchanging either your work or your family. If you are, adjust your time. If the demands of your work cut down on the time you can spend with your family, inform your family. Tell them that a big push is coming up that will require you to put in additional time at work. Explain how long it will take and ask them to understand and bear with you. Tell your family that if, during this time, they need you, you will be there for them, and make sure you are—no matter what.

EVEN BETTER: When demands at work decrease your time with your family, make those periods you spend with them quality time. Ask your family how they want to spend your time together and do what they want.

RULE TWO HUNDRED TWO
VALUE INTEGRITY

The most important quality to seek in others is integrity. Look for it in your employees, associates, and family and social life. Integrity means that a person is highly principled, honest, and will do what he or she promises. You can depend on people with integrity.

WHAT IT MEANS: Life is full of pressures, competing forces that pull people in different directions. Sometimes their compasses drift and they may stray in the wrong direction. When you deal with or rely on people who lack integrity, you can't count on them; you never know what they might do. Since their values waver, even they may not know what they will do. When they're confronted with tough decisions, when doing the "right thing" might be difficult or costly to them, they will usually do what's best for themselves even if it's inconsistent with their purported values and regardless of the impact it might have on others, including you.

ACTION PLAN: Surround yourself with only people of integrity; people whom you believe in and trust. Make your inner core, your closest allies, people of integrity. In hiring, doing business, and your private life, seek and be with only principled individuals. Understand that finding people with integrity can be a hit-and-miss proposition and that your initial impressions can be dead wrong. If that occurs, keep looking for people with integrity.

EVEN BETTER: Be a person of integrity. If you follow your principles, people with integrity will flock to you. They will enhance your life and your business and will enable you to operate on a higher plane.

RULE TWO HUNDRED THREE
Yes Isn't a Dirty Word

Many people are instinctively suspicious; they're cautious doubters who look at everything through a negative lens. Their tendency is to always say no. While being careful can be helpful and keep you from making rash, impulsive decisions, it can often cause you to miss out on wonderful opportunities.

WHAT IT MEANS: In response to whatever they're asked, some people always say no. Although immediately reacting too favorably can make you seem overly eager, always responding with no can be costlier. If they are always turned down, people will no longer ask. They may do it on their own and might do it all wrong or at an inappropriate time. When you constantly reject their proposals, most people will no longer come to you, which can cost you great opportunities. And to further inflame the situation, they may take their projects to your competition or use them to take away your business.

ACTION PLAN: Break the habit of always saying no. Find a comfortable balance between yes and no. Train yourself not to immediately decline. Listen fully, take your time, be fair minded, and examine proposals in greater depth. Then, if you still want to beg off, do so, but only after you have given the request the amount of consideration it deserves.

EVEN BETTER: Extend yourself to people who you have repeatedly rejected. Approach them to solicit their ideas, input, and suggestions. Consider and don't immediately reject their overtures. Show them the new you, a person who is open and won't immediately say no.

PLANS DON'T EXECUTE THEMSELVES

Great accomplishments usually start with great ideas, but simply having a great idea isn't enough to guarantee success. To be successful, it takes much more. At every stage of development, in every detail, you must perform excellently; you must execute.

WHAT IT MEANS: According to the old adage, talk is cheap and ideas are a dime a dozen. Ideas are plentiful; brainstorming, planning, and discussions are important; but ultimately execution, how you get it done, is what counts. Consumers want results; they want what they pay for. When your goods or services don't work, consumers won't be placated by the fact that they were based on good ideas. Although perfecting all the details may not be sexy, fun, or exciting, it can spell the difference between success and failure. Executing your ideas is difficult, which is why they call it work.

ACTION PLAN: Concentrate on the details. Conduct research to find out the best ways to proceed. Hire and consult with the leading experts, the most knowledgeable and experienced authorities in your field. Test, test, test. Put your goods and services under the most rigorous examination, trial by fire, to make sure that they always work under the worst conditions. Set up checkpoints at every stage and don't settle for anything less than the best because consumers won't—at least, not for long.

EVEN BETTER: Put everything in writing. Draft detailed plans and specifications and then write clear explanations that everyone can easily follow. Be exacting—specify the precise dimensions, colors, textures, brands, and results you want, and don't accept less.

RULE TWO HUNDRED FIVE
Magic Formulas Don't Exist

Most problems don't have quick fixes—even though we would love them to. For every card that wins the lottery, millions get tossed in the trash. Hard work plus time is usually the only formula, the only ticket, to success.

WHAT IT MEANS: Everyone wants a shortcut, and why not? If they can find quick ways to make things easier and better, great! Unfortunately, it usually isn't that simple, because most problems are complex. No single answer, action, pill, or magic potion will cure most ills. Sure, sometimes you get lucky and the first thing you try miraculously works. Plus, some matters are relatively easy to mend. However, most took time to develop, and although we want to immediately attack and make them go away, that's not how it tends to work.

ACTION PLAN: Examine every problem that arises and analyze it from every possible angle and every point of view. Try to develop a number of alternative solutions and first try the one that you think has the best chance of working. If it doesn't work, be patient and try to discover why it failed and whether you should make adjustments and try again. When you're convinced that your top alternative will not work, move on to the next possible solution on your list.

EVEN BETTER: Hire experts; experts are the closest things to magic formulas. Experts have vast amounts of knowledge and experience. They have seen most problems and frequently know what will and won't work. And experts also have access to other experts, who may have the answers your expert lacks.

BUDGET YOUR TIME AS WELL AS YOUR MONEY

When we hear the term *budget,* we think in terms of money and how we should allocate it. However, planning how you should spend your time is equally, if not more, important. And the concept of budgeting time is also drastically overlooked.

WHAT IT MEANS: Budgeting your time can be more important than budgeting your money because unlike money, time is not a renewable resource. So, when you spend your time, or worse yet, waste it, you can't get it back. Furthermore, when you waste your time, you don't have anything to show for it. Time gives us the opportunity to make money, but money can't always buy us time.

ACTION PLAN: Place a higher value on your time and how you spend it. Do you spend it on what matters to you most? If not, why? Make a wish list. On that list, state how you most want to spend your time, and don't consider whether you can do so or not. List what you would like to do, not what you realistically can do. Examine your top three to five priorities and see which of them you could achieve. Then create your budget, a schedule that sets aside a precise time for that item or items.

EVEN BETTER: Share you wish list with those closest to you—your wife, husband, partner, children, and/or parents. Let them know how you want to occupy your time, because they may have ideas or suggestions that could help you. Speaking with them could also convince them to budget their time.

RULE TWO HUNDRED SEVEN
SOLVE PROBLEMS BY WORKING BACKWARD

When problems arise, identify the optimum solution you would like to achieve. Then, work back from that solution to where you now are to identify the steps that you can take to solve the problem. Create a map and lay out the best route to your desired destination.

WHAT IT MEANS: A major difficulty in solving problems is seeing them in the right perspective. Often, you're just too close, so the pressure, emotion, and intensity blind you and prevent you from seeing what others find clear. You try to find answers even though you can't see the entire picture and don't have enough information to make an informed decision. If you base your decisions on incomplete information, it's easy to make the wrong decisions and get into deeper trouble.

ACTION PLAN: Pull back; change your perspective. Get an overview so you can clearly see the entire picture. Calm down, diffuse your emotions, and clear your head so that you can think logically and most productively. Examine the possible solutions and identify the one that you want most. Define it specifically by describing in detail exactly what you want. Then, work backward to examine every option, each route you could take. Select the path that seems best, most direct, and has the fewest hurdles. Anticipate obstacles you may encounter and decide how you could bypass or overcome them.

EVEN BETTER: Pick several possible destinations and approaches, prioritize them, and try your top priority first. Create alternatives that you could take at every juncture. Get advice from people whose judgment you trust. Ask them for several options.

Don't Be Afraid to Grow—Its Only Natural

To grow your business, you don't have to change your values or abandon your core ideals. While expansion can change the nature of your business, planning structured around your priorities can enable you to grow and stay true to your ideas.

WHAT IT MEANS: Many business operators fear that if their businesses get bigger, they will never be the same, which is frequently true because when you go forward, you often must leave things behind. So, it's reasonable for them to be concerned that in order to get financing, forge strategic alliances, and operate on a larger scale, they may be forced to make compromises or, worse yet, submit to demands that could be contrary to their own values. Therefore, they move slowly, cautiously, and in doing so, lose opportunities that could have been beneficial to them and their businesses.

ACTION PLAN: Values, like everything else, can change over time. Reevaluate your values to affirm what's most important to you now and what you think will be so in five, ten, and twenty years. Clearly identify your most important values and build your plans to grow around them. Also identify those values that could be lost when you grow, and set up safeguards to preserve those you want to keep.

EVEN BETTER: Communicate your values to everyone you employ and with whom you do business. Strongly impress upon them that retaining your values is your top priority and will not be subject to compromise as you grow. Don't accept the demands of others unless you're convinced that your values will be preserved.

Make Sure Your Umbrella Is Packed When Opportunity Knocks

When opportunities present themselves, you frequently must move fast. If you don't seize them quickly, they can be forever lost. However, by moving fast, you increase the chances of making mistakes. So, prevent disasters by learning as much as you can about what you're going to get into before you dive in.

WHAT IT MEANS: Every decision is risky—no guarantees or sure things exist, so to some extent, every opportunity can be somewhat of a gamble. Smart operators try to cut the risks; they examine opportunities from every angle to spot obstacles that might be involved or that will subsequently arise. In some cases, you won't have enough time or you can't get enough information no matter what you do, but the opportunities may be so great, so lucrative, that they could be worth the risks—whatever they may be.

ACTION PLAN: Educate yourself. Know your industry and those industries related to it inside out so that you always know what is going on and can learn about potential opportunities well before they arise. Build the strongest teams. Identify and forge close relationships with the major players and experts in your and related businesses. Surround yourself with the best, most expert advisors, associates and employees who can give you the wisest, most intelligent counsel when opportunities arise.

EVEN BETTER: Form strategic partnerships and joint ventures with others, especially those who excel in areas in which you may not be as strong. Be willing to pay a premium for their partnership because their expertise, know-how, and connections will usually pay you handsome dividends in time.

RULE TWO HUNDRED TEN
LET YOUR CUSTOMERS VOTE

Although businesses are not democracies, your customers vote—with their wallets. Pay close attention to how your customers cast their votes and make necessary changes accordingly. It could spell the difference between the success or failure of your business.

WHAT IT MEANS: To survive, you must be responsive to your customers. You must know exactly which goods or services your customers are willing to purchase and how much they will pay. Then, your must be able to deliver the goods and services your customers want at prices they will pay. If your customers are pleased with what you offer and feel that you provide good value, they will continue doing business with you. If they are displeased or can get better deals, they will spend their money elsewhere.

ACTION PLAN: Continually monitor your sales and service. Keep detailed and up-to-the-minute records on which items your customers purchase and which they do not. Specifically ask them what they like best about the items they purchase and what they like less. Find out what additional or related products they would buy. Determine why they don't buy your other goods and what changes you could make to land that business.

EVEN BETTER: Bring a representative sampling of your customers into your inner circle. Make them your consultants and advisors. Take them dinner, events, or occasions in exchange for their evaluation of the quality of your goods or services and other benefits they provide. For their help, give them discounts, additional service, training, and the first shot at new items. Unless they request otherwise, credit them widely for the help they provide.

RULE TWO HUNDRED ELEVEN
CHOOSE YOUR BUSINESS BATTLES

In most businesses, annoyances occur each day. In fact, just one annoyance per day wouldn't be half bad. Learning when to speak up and when to remain silent is an art that can be difficult to master—it takes practice, patience, understanding, and restraint.

WHAT IT MEANS: People are imperfect; they act inappropriately and make mistakes. Some of them are just plain irritating; they are hard to work with and have bristly personalities. After a while, it can all mount up. At times, you must speak up to avoid or deal with serious problems; you have no choice. However, on other occasions, it may be best to just shut up because you could make matters worse.

ACTION PLAN: Before you criticize, chastise, or find fault, ask yourself whether the problem could be you. Are you having a bad day, being grouchy or overly sensitive? Then ask yourself if saying anything is necessary. Is the source of your annoyance something that matters or something that you can improve? When you feel yourself growing upset or on the verge of responding strongly, excuse yourself and walk away. Before you leave, politely and calmly explain that you can't deal with this now, but you would like to discuss it later. Don't allow yourself to get drawn into a heated battle.

EVEN BETTER: If you work with difficult people, try to be tolerant and understanding. Speak with them about the problem and try to agree upon solutions. If, after a reasonable time, the problems have not gotten better, the only answer may be for one of you to leave.

MAKE TO-DO LISTS AND MAKE SURE YOU CROSS THEM OFF

It's hard to remember everything, especially if like most businesspeople, you lead a busy, fast-paced life. Don't just trust your memory; get in the habit of making to-do lists in order not to forget important items.

WHAT IT MEANS: Memory is a flawed, unreliable process that is vulnerable to many factors. For example, leading mile-a-minute, high-pressure, and supercharged lives can make it easy for you to overlook things that you wanted to do. In addition, emergencies constantly interrupt at the worst possible times to prevent you from attending to matters that need your attention. As a result, important items get overlooked and fall through the cracks, and when you finally realize that they were neglected, it's usually too late—the damage, which can be substantial, has been done.

ACTION PLAN: Train yourself to make to-do lists. Take the burden off your weary, overworked mind; give it some help. Find a set time each day to make a to-do list. Put all items that you must complete on your list and place them in the most logical, time-efficient order for their completion. Each evening before you retire, review your to-do list for the following day and add to it. First thing the next morning, check your list, and as your day progresses, add new items that must be completed.

EVEN BETTER: Develop systems. Buy a small notebook, a personal digital assistant, or an organizer in which you can write your lists, and carry it on your person. If you keep a written calendar or activities schedule, cross-check it with your to-do list every day.

RULE TWO HUNDRED THIRTEEN
Don't Become a Pack Rat

Things accumulate and before you know it, you can become overwhelmed and surrounded by clutter. So when the time comes, toss out what you no longer use. If you can't remember why something is still taking up space, get rid of it—let it go.

WHAT IT MEANS: Even if you're not a pack rat, stuff has a way of piling up. Papers from who knows when, which you kept for who knows why, may be taking up needed space. Retaining so much limits the room that you have for other items, and it can make it harder to find material that you actually need. Maintaining everything in good condition can also take time, and old papers and books can be fire hazards.

ACTION PLAN: Set aside a specific time every few months to take inventory. Examine those papers, books, and materials that have piled up. Review everything at least once every three months. Set time limits. For instance, discard anything that you haven't referred to in three years that you don't have to retain for legal, tax, or family reasons. Sort everything into three piles: a Yes pile—items you will toss, a No pile—items you will keep, and a Maybe pile—items you will reconsider. Immediately, dispose of everything in the Yes pile. Over the next few months or when you are beginning your next scheduled purge, review the Maybe pile.

EVEN BETTER: Enlist a friend to help you purge; find someone not attached to what you've accumulated. Eliminate everything your helper recommends except five items on which you disagree. Instruct your helper to immediately throw out the eliminated items him- or herself.

TOOT YOUR OWN HORN (BUT DON'T BLARE IT)

Don't be shy about your achievements. Tell others about them, but don't brag, boast, or dominate conversations with your accomplishments. Inform others about what you've accomplished, but be appropriate, humble, and discrete.

WHAT IT MEANS: Most people you meet truly want to know about you; they're usually interested in who you are, what you do, and how it might affect them. Their interest in you may have been aroused by what others have told them, which most probably didn't convey the entire story. Unless, you inform them yourself, they could get the wrong impression and never discover how your needs or interest could connect.

ACTION PLAN: Create a short verbal description that you can recite in the time it takes an elevator to climb from the lobby to the third floor. Keep it between twenty and thirty seconds, with twenty seconds being preferable. In it, say who you are, what you do, and exactly how it can benefit them. Don't boast or brag, simply lay out the facts. Then, have a longer, more explanatory description in reserve that you can provide if they ask you questions. When you speak about yourself, observe the other person's reaction, and the moment he or she wanders, stop talking about yourself.

EVEN BETTER: After making a new acquaintance, exchange business cards. Send an e-mail saying how nice it was to meet and ask if you can send additional material about yourself. Never send unsolicited attachments. Many people resent them and won't open them for fear of viruses.

STUDY THE MASTERS—
THEY GOT THERE FOR A REASON

Learn all you can about the top people in your industry or area of interest as well as leaders in other fields. Study those who have reached the highest plateaus to learn their methods, approaches, and what they did to become so successful. Then try to emulate their success.

WHAT IT MEANS: The individuals who are preeminent in your field, the achievers and thought leaders, probably walked the path you're now following or one quite parallel. In the process, they may have discovered shortcuts and ways to avoid and overcome obstacles. They know, firsthand, what it takes because they blazed the trails; they pioneered the changes and made innovations and breakthroughs that you don't have to reinvent. Learn from their experience; let them be your mentors and teachers.

ACTION PLAN: Identify the people whom you most admire and would like to emulate. Learn all you can about them through books they have written or those that have been written about them. Scour the Internet and magazine racks for articles and profiles by or about them or their businesses and ideas. Read their speeches and interviews. Visit their Web sites, examine their biographies and news releases. Pay close attention to the mistakes they say they made and how they solved or overcame them.

EVEN BETTER: Attend their speeches, lectures, classes, workshops, and seminars. Watch them when they appear on television or the Internet. Listen to when they're on the radio. Go to events where they're present and try to meet them.

RULE TWO HUNDRED SIXTEEN
MOVE FROM BEHIND YOUR DESK

Don't get trapped spending all of your time at work behind your desk. Get up, move around, visit everyone at your workplace and say "hello" to them.

WHAT IT MEANS: With the constant pressure of work and the deadlines that constantly must be met, it's easy to burrow in and let yourself be buried by work, especially when everyone you work with is doing his or her job well. Spending the bulk of your time at your desk can be isolating; it can take you out of the loop and keep you from knowing what's happening in your own business. Remaining at your desk can keep you from developing closer bonds with people at work, and it can make the relationships you do build strictly work oriented, which could be less advantageous in both your business and your life.

ACTION PLAN: Pull yourself away from you desk; leave your office. Leisurely stroll through your workplace. Start casual conversations that are not related to work—stop to spend a few moments and chat. Keep conversations light and pleasant; ask how things are going and pay attention to all responses. Develop friendlier, more personal relationships. Moving around, even for a short while, will help you get some exercise, break the monotony of repetitive work, and refresh your mind.

EVEN BETTER: During meetings, discussions, and interviews, move from behind your desk. Desks can be barriers that impede open talks. They skew the balance of power in favor of the person behind the desk. When you want to have fair exchanges and create win-win situations, move from behind your desk.

RULE TWO HUNDRED SEVENTEEN
THINK LONG TERM

When you make decisions, especially those that could have long-lasting implications, think of your legacy, that is, how you will be regarded years from now for those choices.

WHAT IT MEANS: In making decisions, it's often tempting to just think in the short term and do what's immediately best. Sometimes it's absolutely imperative to close a quick deal or sale because the very survival of your business depends upon it and without it you might have to close shop. However, other considerations may also seep in and cause you to make decisions for questionable reasons. Greed, ego, envy, and impatience can drive you to take actions that move you in the wrong direction, cause you to deal with the wrong people, or take away from your legacy.

ACTION PLAN: Always have a plan and follow it. Build your plan around your values. Project your plan well into the future, for at least five to ten years. When you're faced with decisions, balance your immediate needs with what you, or those who follow you, might need or want someday. Examine your options from a perspective of ten, twenty, and thirty years from now. Ask if the decisions you're about to make might compromise your values.

EVEN BETTER: Before you finalize decisions, ask yourself how you would explain them to your great-grandchildren. Could you tell them the truth? Would they understand and take pride in the choices you made? What, as a result of this decision, would you be leaving to your grandchildren?

SEIZE OPPORTUNITIES, THEN FIGURE THEM OUT

In business, you must capitalize on opportunities, breaks that could enable you to advance more closely to your goals. Learn to recognize these openings, and when they arise, jump on them even though you may not know exactly how you're going to proceed.

WHAT IT MEANS: Great opportunities don't occur every day. When they arise, you may have to move fast before other, more powerful and resourceful competitors learn about them and try to get involved. Since opportunities can arise suddenly, you may be caught off guard because you have not figured out all of the details on how you can make it work. However, if you wait to act until you have worked out every little detail, you may be too late. Your big chance may pass and you may never get the opportunity again.

ACTION PLAN: Always be alert to opportunities; consciously look for them. Hone your instincts and polish your ability to recognize possibilities that could help your business or career. Trust your knowledge and understanding of your business. Don't be rash or overly impulsive, but also don't be overly cautious. Examine each situation and evaluate your risks; quantify exactly what you have to lose and decide how much you're willing to risk.

EVEN BETTER: Cultivate the best, smartest, and most experienced advisors; experts who you can always call on to give you the soundest advice. Find great people who know the pulse of your industry and can help you with the details or refer you to others who can.

RULE TWO HUNDRED NINETEEN
IT'S NOT ALWAYS ABOUT MONEY (NO, *REALLY*!)

Since business is about making money, business decisions tend to turn on the costs, savings, and profits involved. However, other considerations can be equally or even more important. For example, it may be wise to pay a premium to purchase an item if the seller will give you long-term financing at a low rate, especially if your purchase will probably increase in value.

WHAT IT MEANS: Money is the standard of measurement. Businesses are usually judged on how much money they make and on their profitability. While these criteria may be valid for evaluating large corporations, they may not be appropriate for every business decision. Everyone has different values and objectives. For some, being able to spend more time with their family or to work at home or in a business they love may trump higher wages. Others may prefer to work for less in order to learn; put in fewer hours; or get experience, benefits, and greater opportunities.

ACTION PLAN: Identify your objectives for both the short and long term. Include timelines for attaining each stage of your goals. Clearly understand exactly what you want from a job, business, or career—the precise reasons you're there. Set your priorities and then create a plan of action because once you know what you want, your goals will be easier to reach.

EVEN BETTER: If you're uncertain about certain decisions, quantify how much the cost of achieving your goals would be worth to you. Examine whether the cost of getting experience, having time with your family, or having more time to stay at home is worth the lower salary you would be paid.

THINK LIKE AN INDEPENDENT OPERATOR

Jobs are no longer secure, and people don't spend entire careers at the same job or with the same company. At times, it may be best to consider yourself an independent operator who is under contract to provide services to the business that pays you.

WHAT IT MEANS: Over the last decade, the business climate has changed. Corporations, including the biggest multinational conglomerates, are now routinely bought and sold. U.S. business that were household names have merged, been taken over, and are called by different names. Some have foreign ownership. As the business landscape changed, so has the underlying relationship between businesses and their employees. Companies seldom feel a sense of loyalty or obligation to their employees. Job security is ancient history, as are pensions and free health care.

ACTION PLAN: If a business employs you full-time, think of yourself as an independent business operator, not as a part of the company that pays you. Enjoy your salary, enjoy the benefits, but understand that your first priority must be yourself and your career. View every task you perform, challenge you master, tactic you devise, deal you close, person you manage as an entry for your resume, a deposit in your experience account that you can take to the bank and cash in.

EVEN BETTER: Be loyal to your company; do the work you're paid for and do it excellently. Build your value within the business; make it dependent on you. Learn the skills to run your own business, and when you leave, part on good terms and convince your ex-employer to contract your duties out to you.

RULE TWO HUNDRED TWENTY-ONE
MAKE A DIFFERENCE, NO MATTER WHAT YOU DO

Whatever you do, try to do it better than it's previously been done. Always try to add, improve, contribute, and elevate. Set new standards and don't live your life or perform your work at the levels others have established; make your own mark.

WHAT IT MEANS: Some workers are content just completing the assignments they're given; they do the bare minimum, nothing more and nothing less. They see their work as just a job, so they do as little as possible. Then they wonder why they don't feel fulfilled. Invariably, they become bored by the repetition of their jobs or frustrated by the fact that they're not asked to take on anything new or exciting, or selected for advancement. Usually, they don't last, and before long, they're gone.

ACTION PLAN: Do the best you can and always look for new ways to do things better. Challenge and stimulate yourself by taking on harder problems or finding new approaches or routes; otherwise, you may run the risk of boring yourself to death. Impress your bosses, colleagues, and associates with your initiative, your desire to constantly improve. Treat what you attempt as important; give it dignity, stature, and worth because when you do, others will appreciate your efforts and regard you with admiration and respect.

EVEN BETTER: Volunteer your services. Find opportunities to use your skills to help others who are less fortunate and could use a hand. Let them share in your good fortune. Show them through your example how to improve their lot. Perhaps someday, they will pass the torch by giving their help to others.

RULE TWO HUNDRED TWENTY-TWO
HOOK UP WITH SOUL MATES

Most achievements are more satisfying when you accomplish them with others. And they're even more fulfilling when you share them with those who subscribe to your visions and beliefs. Enlist others to join you on your journey; it can make the trip quicker, more enjoyable, and more successful.

WHAT IT MEANS: At its pinnacle, life is a collaborative experience. Virtually all experiences have greater meaning when you share them with other special individuals. Working on projects with those who are close is simply more fun, and it's usually more productive. When each of you takes on the burden and performs the work, the accomplishments become more enjoyable, the obstacles easier to overcome, and the payoffs richer. Collaboration is an unparalleled teacher that can lift you higher than you can reach by yourself; it can open new doors by introducing you to new ideas and perspectives.

ACTION PLAN: Go to places where you can meet individuals with similar interests and ambitions. Talk to people. Openly discuss your ideas and objectives. Find out all about them—their backgrounds, interests, and plans; exchange thoughts, learn how they think and act. Trust your instincts and your reactions. Build on your excitement and enthusiasm. Seize opportunities to form close ties with those with whom you can share your dreams.

EVEN BETTER: When you find soul mates, meet their friends and associates, explore their worlds. Expand your base; build your network and team. Put yourself in a position to be continually meeting new and exciting people.

RULE TWO HUNDRED TWENTY-THREE
LET OTHERS TAKE THE SPOTLIGHT

To rise within an organization, subdue your ego; step into the shadows, out of the spotlight, and let others take the credit. Attach yourself to an outstanding, up-and-coming individual—lets call him or her your patron. Support your patron's ambitions and keep a low profile. By being a good soldier and letting your patron have the glory, you can work your way straight up to the top.

WHAT IT MEANS: Never lose sight of the ego factor. For many people, especially business leaders, ego is one of the major motivators that drive them to succeed. Understand that these individuals feed on compliments and constantly need recognition, which is why they push themselves and everyone else so hard. When they become successful, their egos help to keep them on top. Therefore, if they see you as a threat, they may act to protect themselves and stop you in your tracks.

ACTION PLAN: When you're working with others, always assume that they have a big ego that constantly must be stroked. Leave the stroking to others because coming from you, it usually will be too transparent, no matter how subtle you try to be. Instead, work diligently to support patron success and let others lavish him or her with praise. Hitch yourself to your patron's star and become a part of his or her success. Stay in the background, but don't be resentful; be smart, be pleasant, and be patient. Your turn will come.

EVEN BETTER: Look for opportunities to get your patron recognition. Then, tell your patron about them and let him or her decide how to proceed and what role he or she wants you to play.

RULE TWO HUNDRED TWENTY-FOUR
ENCOURAGE NEW IDEAS FROM DIFFERENT SOURCES

When new ideas are presented, be encouraging even if a particular suggestion has no merit or is untimely, inappropriate, or unrealistic. Make it your objective to create a culture in which ideas are prized and the fact that they are presented is more important than the quality of any specific idea.

WHAT IT MEANS: To some degree, all businesses are internally territorial. Most employees want to protect their own turf and hang on to what they have. Therefore, they can be resistant to any movement toward change. When new ideas are put forward, they may be closed to all suggestions, even those that could help them and bring positive change. They may also be cynical, petty, and overly critical regarding the best of ideas. Frequently, these organizations get bogged down within their own structures and suffocated by the very barriers they erect.

ACTION PLAN: Encourage and place a premium on new ideas and suggestions. Create an environment in which new thinking is not only encouraged, but is rewarded by acknowledgments, promotions, and bonuses. At least twice each month, hold idea and brainstorming meetings. Make these meetings casual and informal and tell everyone not to hold back. Encourage them to be silly, irreverent, impractical, unrealistic, and over the top. Make it clear that no idea or suggestion is too trivial, weak, or embryonic to be proposed.

EVEN BETTER: Invite a mix of employees from every facet of your business to idea and brainstorming sessions. To make these meetings even more productive, bring in your customers, suppliers, vendors, and people who are authorities on a variety of subjects.

LISTEN TO DISSENTERS—THEY MAY KNOW WHAT THEY'RE TALKING ABOUT

When others disagree with you, pay attention to their opinions. Regardless of the source, no matter who it is, don't get defensive and dismiss contrary views before you fully understand the basis of their different points of view.

WHAT IT MEANS: Divergent opinions can be the last thing you want to hear, especially when you're gripped by the excitement of new ideas or ventures. When others find fault with something you believe in, it can be demoralizing, discouraging, and deflating. Disagreement can be particularly unwelcome when offered by contrarians, folks who always seem to take the opposing sides of arguments. However, the fact that they regularly dissent doesn't mean that their objections don't have merit.

ACTION PLAN: Put your ideas to the most severe tests. Welcome the most intense challenges in order to prove the soundness of your ideas. When you disagree with dissenters, give credence to their thinking and try to understand it. Understand that others may share their views, and they may be an enlightened minority. Be open to the possibility that they could be right and see flaws that others could not detect. Fully investigate their fears and see what changes you could implement that would allay their feelings. Finally, consider whether you are presenting your ideas convincingly, because your manner of communication could be the source of the problem and their negative reactions.

EVEN BETTER: Welcome scrutiny and encourage dissent. Conduct meetings expressly for your colleagues, employees, and associates to challenge your ideas, approaches, and decisions. Make these challenges a part of your business process, which ideas have to overcome in order to be developed.

RULE TWO HUNDRED TWENTY-SIX
CHALLENGE EACH OF YOUR ASSUMPTIONS

Never assume—verify everything. Conduct research to support each and every facet of your decision-making process or your business could collapse as a result of being built on a foundation of incorrect assumptions.

WHAT IT MEANS: Everyone makes assumptions based on information that he or she honestly believes; people jump to conclusions that are often incorrect. Frequently, they make conclusions on items or information with which they're familiar but have never actually substantiated or checked. An experienced salesperson may assume that a large market exists for a certain product, that women will love it and buy it for gifts. A personnel specialist may conclude that great salespersons can be hired within a reasonable salary range. Mistakes are often made in situations when assumptions seem so obvious that they're never checked.

ACTION PLAN: List all your assumptions. Break down every piece of each item and step; consider nothing too small or insignificant to check. Before you invest any effort or resources, examine each of your beliefs on which you have based or will base any decision, to confirm that they're true. Since everything continually changes, constantly recheck your assumptions and be sure that they remain correct. When any of your assumptions proves untrue, go back to the drawing board. Rethink your plans and implement new approaches that are based on the information that you verified.

EVEN BETTER: Hire consultants to examine your assumptions. Understand that you may be too close to your ideas, processes, and ambitions to identify all of your assumptions and to check whether they're correct. Assign members of your staff to assist the consultants you employ.

KEEP YOUR FOOT
ON THE GAS PEDAL

When you meet your goals, don't sit back and congratulate yourself; keep driving forward. When you're on a roll, use the momentum from your achievements to implement new initiatives that can launch you to even greater successes.

WHAT IT MEANS: After assignments or projects have been successfully realized, it's natural to want to take some time to relax. A pause may be necessary in order for you to reenergize and rebuild resources that you spent. Sometimes, however, these interludes continue far too long; you can get trapped by inertia and not want to move. Suddenly, projects that were once far off require your attention, and deadlines loom. So, you have to dive right in and rush like mad to get them completed. This can force you to put added pressure on your team and may diminish your chances of doing a first-rate job.

ACTION PLAN: If you take a break, keep it short. Then, be prepared to move while you're still on top, while you're operating at maximum efficiency and top speed. Get back into action. Let the elation from your success fuel your next ventures. Use that excitement to rally all the members of your team and people with whom you will be working. Encourage them to try even harder and achieve even better results.

EVEN BETTER: Instead of taking a break, jump right into new projects without any delay. However, build time into the new projects for you and your teammates to regularly rest and recharge.

RULE TWO HUNDRED TWENTY-EIGHT
SCOUT YOUR COMPETITION— THEY'RE SCOUTING YOU

To reach and stay on top, you must be an expert on your field or industry. You must be an authority on your business and your entire industry, including your competition. Know what your competition is doing—the quality of their goods, services, and operating procedures as well as how they compare to yours.

WHAT IT MEANS: All businesses are vulnerable; even monopolies crumble. With the advent of technology and globalization, enterprising innovators are finding better, cheaper, and more efficient ways to undercut even the most well-established and highly regarded business. In our shrunken world, the most serious threat to your business may be located on the other side of the globe, below the radar. So, to stay on top, you must know your industry, all the players, actual and potential competitors.

ACTION PLAN: Create an ongoing program to know and keep abreast of your industry. Meet and get to know all of the experts, movers and shakers, and thought leaders. Subscribe to industry papers and materials and attend industry events. Question your suppliers, vendors, and customers about your competitors and how their goods and services compare with yours. Purchase and order competitors' goods and products and test them. Evaluate them for yourself, dissect them, and take them apart to fully understand how they work. Anticipate your competitors' future moves and identify others who could become your competitors.

EVEN BETTER: Hire the top consultants in your industry to analyze the competition and the quality of their goods, services, and business operations in comparison to yours. Have them identify potential competitors and help you devise strategies to counter their threats.

TACKLE THE TOUGHEST JOBS

Show that you have broad shoulders by volunteering for the most difficult assignments. Demonstrate your talent and show that you're an invaluable team player by willingly performing jobs that no one else wants to do.

WHAT IT MEANS: In every business, certain tasks must be completed that no one wants to do. Many people see them as the dirty work or assignments that are beneath them regardless of how essential to the business they may be. Sometimes, they're just plain hard or messy or they force you to work with unpleasant people, places, and things. So, most others will try to avoid them and palm them off. They may also ridicule or belittle those who are forced to perform them. However, the mere fact that you are willing to attempt hard and/or unpleasant jobs will impress those who count the most and will boost your career.

ACTION PLAN: Distinguish yourself by taking on undesirable assignments, and when you successfully complete them, volunteer for more. Create a pattern of tackling the most difficult jobs; be cheerful, positive, and show your willingness to do what others shun. Expect it to take a while for key people to notice your accomplishments, but eventually they will. And when they do, they usually will show new respect for you and position you for greater rewards.

EVEN BETTER: When you take on the dirty work, never complain, and perform those jobs excellently, better than anyone else has. When you successfully complete them, downplay your achievements. Don't blow your own horn, just quietly complete the job and move on.

GET A SECOND OPINION

Never make important decisions alone; always get at least one other opinion from someone you respect. Surround yourself with the brightest, most experienced and objective experts in every phase of your business. Find people who will always give you sound advice, and don't commit to matters of importance without consulting them.

WHAT IT MEANS: Although the job description for a leader lists decision making as a prime requirement, important determinations should not be made alone. Of course, leaders are ultimately responsible for every decision; they must always make the final call. But acting in isolation generally isn't wise, and it often is just plain stupid. Even when you're pressed for time, especially when you're pressed for time, it's vital to collect all the best information and listen to learned voices in order to take the right course of action.

ACTION PLAN: Locate the most intelligent and experienced individuals in all areas connected to your business. Call them your board of directors, your advisors, your mentors, or your team. Select individuals who are exceptionally bright, highly experienced, independent thinkers, and well connected. They must understand your business and your objectives and not be afraid to disagree with you or your other advisors. Make sure that you always have quick access to them.

EVEN BETTER: Pay your advisors appropriately for their access and advice. Understand that the best information and advice are expensive, if you can even buy them, and having them readily available to you is worth a premium. This will show your appreciation and encourage top advisers to continue to support you.

Have More Than Three Plays in the Playbook

All people and situations can't always be treated alike. What works wonders with one individual or state of affairs may not work for another. So, be flexible and treat each person and situation according to what seems most likely to achieve the best results.

WHAT IT MEANS: Leaders, managers, and administrators can be stubborn; they can get trapped in their own perceptions of their identity and refuse to budge. "That's who I am and that's how I do things," they may declare. Often they feel that because they're in charge, they have to stand firm, and if they treat people and matters differently, they will be considered inconsistent and lose control. Many insist that that their methods are well proven and have been so successful that others, rather than they, must change.

ACTION PLAN: Adapt to different people and challenges; become flexible. One answer, one method, doesn't fit all. People don't think or respond in the same way: pushing Employee A may produce great results, but applying those same tactics could devastate Employee B. In addition, what worked wonders yesterday may fall flat today simply because slightly different timing, factors, or individuals are involved.

EVEN BETTER: Don't be constrained by rules; keep them to the bare minimum. People and conditions constantly change, so rules can suddenly be out of date. Enforcing outdated, inapplicable rules is senseless and can force you to make counterproductive decisions. Instead, cut down on your rules and deal with different people and situations on an individual basis.

Knowing Your Worth Will Help You Get It

Before you sell your services, know precisely what they're worth. Survey the market and learn how much you can expect to receive for each of the services you offer, and the ceilings that some potential customers or clients will pay. Don't jump at great-sounding offers before you know what your services are worth.

WHAT IT MEANS: If you don't know your value, you may ask for more than potential customers or clients are willing to pay. So, at some point, you'll probably have to lower your price. This can drag out the process, cost you both time and money, and make you look unprofessional. If you charge too little for your services, you will eventually resent underpricing yourself because you will be working too hard or too much for too little. This usually fosters frustration, irritation, and even resentment, which can interfere with your efforts and the quality of the services you provide.

ACTION PLAN: Prior to entering the market, identify those who are providing similar services. Then, find out how much they are being paid. Contact headhunters and survey a broad spectrum of people and situations to find a price range. When you feel that you know the market, develop a sales strategy. For example, you might decide to initially ask for less in order to get your foot in the door, to receive a strong benefits package, to work near home, to have flexible hours, or to have assurances of continuing work.

EVEN BETTER: Note which businesses pay the most for the services you provide and find out exactly why. Then, offer those premium items to increase the compensation you can receive.

Keep Your Moving Boxes, You May Need Them

Frequently, the best way to fast-forward your career is to move to a new job, firm, or area. Sometimes, it's the only route because you may have hit the ceiling as far as what you can learn, what you can earn, and where you can rise.

WHAT IT MEANS: Many businesses don't try to help their employees' careers. They only want them to do their work and they have little interest in their futures or their growth. In one business, you can be stuck forever in the same position, with no place to go. Frequently, the only way to ascend to a higher level is to go with another company or firm; by moving laterally, you can move up. Furthermore, businesses in other locations often offer more compensation and career opportunities than those in your own backyard do.

ACTION PLAN: No matter how much you like your job or present situation, be open to other opportunities. Better yet, always know what other opportunities exist. Speak with headhunters. Even if you don't apply for other jobs, knowing the market will strengthen your hand with your present employer and clarify what you must do to grow and progress. Since moving can be disruptive to families, discuss moving with your spouse, partner, and/or family. Together, clarify your priorities so that if opportunities arise, you can make the best decision for all of you.

EVEN BETTER: While breaking old bonds can be traumatic, it can also be liberating and uplifting. Adjust your attitude. Think of change as entering, not as leaving; as a positive growth experience that will add to, rather than detract from, your and your family's life.

No One Is Indispensable

We all can be replaced, eliminated, done without. As invaluable as we think we are, others may not agree. They may think, and correctly so, that the business will run better and/or more profitably without us.

WHAT IT MEANS: Even if you started the business, mortgaged everything to finance it, built it from scratch, and it bears your name, it can continue without you. It happens all the time! Your business may run better under your daughter, your son, your son-in-law, the new corporate owners, or those investors who are trying to force you out. Although your business may have been born from your vision and built with your love, energy, and drive, it's still just a business and can thrive under other people's love, energy, and drive.

ACTION PLAN: Pull back; don't totally merge your identity with your business. No matter how much you love your business and how proud you are of its success, understand that it is not all you are. Instead of thinking of it as your life, think of it as a fabulous learning experience, a great accomplishment, and a beautiful phase in your life. Take pride in it and continue to give it your full effort, but understand that someday you may have to pull away. And when that day comes, you want to be ready to begin new ventures and achieve new goals.

EVEN BETTER: Don't hang on. Know your limits and when to retreat. Involve yourself in activities and interests outside of your business so you can gracefully retreat. Find other outlets for your drive, ambitions, and pride and throw yourself into them.

LEARN FROM DEFEAT— YOU'LL SEE IT AGAIN

Losses and defeats are inevitable; no one wins every time. However, losses don't have to be complete wipeouts; they can be beneficial if you take something valuable from them.

WHAT IT MEANS: Everything isn't just black or white, good or bad, win or lose. Many shades or gradients lie between each extreme. All your endeavors will not succeed. Some will fail; let's hope that they're not many. To grow, develop, and learn, it's essential to salvage lessons from both your victories and defeats, to obtain nurturing information, insights, and experiences that you can apply to future endeavors to help you to obtain greater gains.

ACTION PLAN: When you don't succeed, examine if anything in the ashes could still have some use or value. It frequently will. When someone turns you down, ask if he or she might be interested at a later time, how you could improve your candidacy, and if he or she knows others who could be interested in you. Consider whomever your speak with, meet, and interact with to be a contact. Cultivate those contacts; bring them into your network. Always leave on a positive note by thanking them for their time, consideration, and any help that they could give you. Follow up by e-mail, a note, and an occasional message simply to maintain the contact. Send them information, tell them of your successes, and thank them for any inspiration they may have provided or roles they may have played.

EVEN BETTER: Look for opportunities where you probably won't succeed but that could give you helpful experience, contacts, information, or visibility. Concentrate on increasing your knowledge, exposure, and network rather than just getting onetime or short-term wins.

RULE TWO HUNDRED THIRTY-SIX
NO ONE WILL SELL YOU MORE AGGRESSIVELY THAN YOU

Ultimately, most business matters come down to sales. If you want to advance your position or achieve your agenda, you must convince those in power of the worthiness of your proposal. And you can't do it halfheartedly or assume that they will recognize the merits of your plan. Show them, convince them, sell.

WHAT IT MEANS: What may seem abundantly clear to you may be a complete mystery to others; what you see as the most brilliant, innovative, and necessary ideas may leave others scratching their heads. Even when they get it and fully understand the value of what you propose, give them more—additional or stronger reasons that will justify their decision to do as you recommend. Be thorough and leave nothing to chance.

ACTION PLAN: Create a detailed sales plan for every pitch, proposal, and overture you present. First, test your ideas on people you respect. In the process, you will be enlisting key people who can guide you and support your plan. Decide whom to approach first and what to say. Cover all the bases by soliciting their opinions, objections, and suggestions. Learn what potential problems they see and how they can be avoided. Find out what additional research, analysis, and testing must be completed and if they know of better alternatives. When you have the answers, prepare demonstrations, prototypes, and visual aids to support your pitch. Practice your presentation until you know that you can convincingly answer any questions and counter all objections.

EVEN BETTER: Compile facts and figures in support of your plan. Put them in monetary terms. Document the precise profits to be expected, the losses to be reversed, and the growth that will be achieved.

RULE TWO HUNDRED THIRTY-SEVEN
BE ASSERTIVE—BUT NOT AGGRESSIVE

Assertiveness in the workplace is essential for several reasons. First and foremost, it's about being able to appropriately communicate your ideas and stand up for yourself. Second, it's one of the keys to garnering respect. And finally, it adds to your visibility and authenticity. Too many people keep quiet even when their ideas might be very valuable, or they suffer unwarranted criticism in stoic silence when they might do better to speak up.

WHAT IT MEANS: Being assertive means behaving in a direct and honest way and not faking what you think or feel in order to be liked. Many people confuse assertiveness with being demanding and pushy—even manipulative. Wrong! Appropriate assertiveness is saying what you think—even if it will sometimes rock the boat. It's having the courage to express your convictions, but in a polite and professional way. It could mean telling someone that his or her behavior is unacceptable—without name-calling. Paying a genuine compliment is assertive—positively assertive. Even silence can be assertive, such as when you refuse to laugh at an offensive joke.

ACTION PLAN: Think about whether there are any situations or relationships at work that might benefit from your being more assertive. What might you say—and how do you think the other person might react? Realize that challenging the status quo is always risky, so decide whether this particular battle is worth fighting. Also, resolve to more regularly weigh in with your opinion—without regard for its potential popularity. You won't always get your way, of course, but at least you'll have your say.

EVEN BETTER: Learn how to deal effectively with inappropriately assertive people. Stay calm, describe the behavior that you find objectionable, and state what you want and/or intend to do. For example, "If you're unwilling to lower your voice and speak in a normal manner, I refuse to continue this conversation." Or, "I don't know whether you're intentionally trying to be insulting or not, but I don't appreciate it—and I don't intend to continue this conversation unless you stop. Am I clear?" Asking the other person a question can be an effective strategy because it invites the person to stop and think—and possibly change his or her behavior.

Market to the Smallest Possible Large Group

No business can be everything to everybody, and it's dumb to try—because your marketing message will lack credibility. What you need to do is develop a message that appeals to the wants and needs of a specific market segment. Marketing works best when it reaches the right market with the right message at the right time.

WHAT IT MEANS: Compelling marketing messages should evoke that "Aha—this is exactly what I need!" reaction in readers or listeners, so your challenge is twofold. First, figure out your target customer profile as best as you can—what are his or her "hot buttons" and what is it about your product/service that will push them? Then, you need to plan a program that will help you regularly communicate this message to your target audience as effectively as possible. A direct mail or e-mail campaign might be more cost-effective than a TV or radio spot. It doesn't pay to reach a mass audience of two million if your real target market is just 200,000 and can be reached more efficiently through another medium.

ACTION PLAN: Conduct the marketing and media research to pinpoint your most promising target market(s) and pursue them. This will not only help you develop more on-target market forecasts and plans, it will help you (or your ad people) create more effective marketing materials. Too many ads suffer from being 100 percent "product-centric" and thus fail to speak to the hearts and minds of prospective customers.

EVEN BETTER: You can't be all things to all people, but you can emphasize different features and benefits to different markets ... and perhaps you should. Consider the value of developing an advertising campaign geared to a secondary market. How would your message need to be changed? How would you attempt to reach that market? Like the best baseball pitchers, your marketing results may end up in the winner's column more often if you develop more than one good "pitch."

To Every Business There Is A Season

Your talent, strategies, and plans can certainly affect the results of your efforts, but they can't control it. General economic conditions—recessions and booms—will impact your business, but you can do something more positive to survive and thrive during the leaner times than merely complain.

WHAT IT MEANS: A robust economy can often compensate (and then some) for many managerial mistakes. No matter what you do, or so it seems, the cash register keeps ringing, and your business keeps growing, year after year ... but not forever. All boom cycles come to an end, and steering your business through a recession can indeed be challenging. Clearly, you have much less of a margin for error. On the other hand, you have an opportunity to prove your mettle as a manager, to be more prudent and more resourceful, and to pursue certain strategies that can strengthen your company, recession or not. You can complain all you want about how bad business is, and you will undoubtedly have plenty of company willing to commiserate with you, but the bottom line is that complaining does absolutely no good for your bottom line.

ACTION PLAN: First, keep your finger on the pulse of general economic trends by reading the business section of your newspaper or a good business magazine. Second, realize that the fundamentals of managing a business still apply during a recession—perhaps more so than ever. You need to cut costs and improve operating efficiency. Explore how you can make do with less. Now may be a good time to let go of nonessential workers or switch to temps or independent contractors ... or to explore outsourcing options.

EVEN BETTER: Like Duke Ellington once said, every problem is a chance for you to do your best. The challenge to keep your business going during tough times can be highly motivating. Now is the time to work your network and more aggressively seek referrals. Now may be a favorable time to negotiate better prices from your suppliers or landlord. Now may be a good time to emphasize the economical benefits of your products or services. Also, realize that most recessions are not global—there are usually some industries and regions that remain unaffected—so perhaps now might be an advantageous time to explore potential new markets.

Use Bundling to Increase Perceived Value—and Sales

An effective way to increase your profits and sales is to bundle many products or services together into one package. This gives people more reasons to buy your products and services. People also have come to believe package deals are a better value—especially when the total package costs less than the sum of its parts.

WHAT THIS MEANS: Bundling works for a very simple but compelling reason: people always like the idea of getting more for their money. The trick is to make your products or services closely related. For example, if you're selling a computer, you could add in software, hardware, installation, maintenance, computer furniture, et cetera. Bundling can also increase your target markets, which in return would give you a larger audience to sell your products and services to. For example, if you're selling a baseball magazine, you could add a free baseball when someone buys a subscription. You're now targeting people who want the baseball magazine and those who want to play baseball out in the yard. Some people will buy a package deal just to get one of the products.

ACTION PLAN: There are many ways to go about choosing the right products or services to bundle into one package. You could survey your customers and see what products or services they would like you to offer in the future. Spy on your competition to discover what products and services they're offering or not offering. If you would like to bundle unrelated products or services together, ask your customers which ones would be of interest to them.

EVEN BETTER: One size bundle does not necessarily fit all, so consider offering various price points—such as "value," "standard," and "king-sized." Giving customers this kind of a choice—between yes and yes—usually generates more sales than choices between yes and no, because you're enabling them to choose something more in sync with their budget and needs.

TOUR YOUR OWN WEB SITE

If your Web site isn't making it easier for you to market and sell your products/ services, then it's probably getting in the way. Your customers won't bother telling you—they'll be gone in a few moments and clicks—so you owe it to your company's marketing well-being to conduct an impartial and comprehensive site inspection of your own.

WHAT IT MEANS: Your Web site can be an amazingly effective marketing tool, but only if it's useful and user-friendly. All the great content in the world will matter not a whit if users are confused about how to navigate your site or are bombarded by glitzy animations and other special effects or are simply overwhelmed by information overload. Your first priority should be to find out if your site is as easy to navigate as you think it is. Don't ask your webmaster or marketing people—they are most likely to tell you what you want to hear. Ask friends (or friendly customers) who are unfamiliar with your site to find a particular piece of information on it, then listen carefully to their experience and revise accordingly. Keep your top-level navigation broad, and let visitors "drill down" to the next level—but keep those levels to a minimum. Visitors shouldn't have to click more than three times to reach the information they seek. If you provide a search function, make sure your search results are relevant and that they provide enough information for visitors to determine where to go next.

ACTION PLAN: Here are the top ten things your customers are looking for on your Web site:

- Contact information
- Product information
- Samples of products (or previous work)
- Support (troubleshooting assistance, FAQs, etc.)
- E-commerce ability (can they buy online?)
- Company information
- News and announcements

- Employment opportunities
- An easy way to get back to your home page
- Intuitively simple navigation

If any of these criteria are missing or in need of improvement, make it a top priority to take care of it.

EVEN BETTER: The more useful your Web site is to its visitors, the more valuable it will be to you. Consider offering white papers, special reports, video clip product demos, special "Web only" introductory offers, et cetera. Also, consider programs that will drive more traffic to your Web site, such as e-mail marketing, press releases, postcard promos, et cetera.

RULE TWO HUNDRED FORTY-TWO
Everyone Has a Web Site— Make the Most of Yours

Chances are that you're doing things via the Internet to improve your productivity or get better value than you were just a few years ago—and chances are just as good (probably even better) that you've only touched the tip of the iceberg!

WHAT IT MEANS: The Internet can help you pinpoint information in ways above and beyond your current usage—so stay curious and open to new ways that the Internet, both personally and professionally, can be of benefit. For example, many people use Google or another search engine to locate information on competitors, business trends, new products—virtually anything. You can use a travel portal (Orbitz.com, Expedia.com, priceline.com) to save money on transportation, car rentals, and lodging. You can buy books, slightly used, at savings of 50 percent or more at amazon.com. You can get great deals on office supplies, PCs, and electronics on eBay or by doing a quick Web-wide price comparison at Froogle.com; hire local talent at craigslist.com; get directions at MapQuest.com—and that's just off the top of my head! The point is that many practical and valuable needs can be greatly facilitated and accommodated online. The challenge is to know about them.

ACTION PLAN: Stay curious and learn more about what's new and possible by talking to colleagues or reading books, newspapers, or PC magazines. For example, a recent article in *PC World* (July 2005) listed "30 Things You Didn't Know You Could Do on the Internet"—including getting free technical help, creating and distributing e-mail newsletters, reminding yourself about special events or things to do, hiring a virtual office manager, or conducting business meetings online. Learn more at *www.pcworld.com*.

EVEN BETTER: Use the Internet to help you learn more about whatever you want to know. Brush up on your online research skills (there's a bit more to it than Google), and the Internet can become your 24/7 library, concierge, shopping mall, and business intelligence consultant.

Systematically Seek Referrals

What's the quickest way to build your business? Ask most professional marketers, and they'll tell you adopting a referral program is the preferred route to increased sales. Referrals are your hottest prospects because they come to you ready to buy. But you can't sit back hoping customers and associates will send the right referral prospects your way. To keep a steady stream of referrals coming in, you'll need a dedicated marketing program designed for that purpose.

WHAT IT MEANS: A good referral is more likely to create a customer than any slick brochure or advertising campaign, and your costs are relatively nil—so don't leave your referral acquisition efforts to chance. Start by communicating regularly with your current and past customers to stay "top of mind." Use electronic newsletters, broadcast faxes or direct mail, and telephone calls to maintain relationships and generate referrals. If you work with clients or customers on a project basis, distribute a survey or follow-up letter including a request for referrals at the completion of every project. Next, identify the types of businesses that influence your customers' or clients' buying decisions or that market complementary products or services to your target audience. For example, if you own a roofing company, insurance agents may be good referral sources for homeowners whose roofs have been damaged by fallen trees or storms. Focus on your referral prospects and build a targeted marketing program using the aforementioned tactics.

ACTION PLAN: Create specialized marketing tools. For example, a mortgage brokerage might print mortgage calculation sheets with its company name and logo and distribute them to real estate agents to use when meeting with prospective home buyers.

Consider offering your referral sources incentives (gifts). Keep in mind that referrals are a two-way street. If you're ever in a position to refer business to your referral sources, make sure to let them know about it.

EVEN BETTER: One of the cardinal rules of successful referral relationships is to always keep those who send you referrals up-to-date on the outcome. Train everyone who answers your incoming calls from prospects to ask callers where they heard about your company, and track this information in your marketing database. Create a basic thank-you letter that you and your staff can personalize and send as a follow-up to each referral you receive. Handle all referrals with the utmost care, and you'll build a foundation of trust that will ensure the success of your referral marketing program and keep those hot prospects coming in.

RULE TWO HUNDRED FORTY-FOUR
SOME TRENDS MIGHT JUST BE FADS— BE CAREFUL WHOM YOU FOLLOW

Few "tools" are more widely abused these days than so-called best practices. It's no wonder that most banks, supermarkets, airlines, retailers, and professional services firms look astonishingly similar—they've been busy copying each other's best practices for decades. *Best practices* has joined the long list of meaningless phrases like *scalable strategies, seamless integration,* and *transformational initiatives.* Whenever a business buzzword has degenerated into a ubiquitous cliché, it's best taken with a grain of salt—if at all.

WHAT IT MEANS: Is there value in learning from the experience and success of others? Of course! Many organizations are saddled with similar challenges, so copying may seem like the ultimate shortcut to salvation. The problem with best practices is that you might blithely assume that they can be successfully transplanted within your organization—and that can be a very costly mistake! Starting any project with a canned solution stifles the innovation customers expect from their suppliers. When you import best practices, the team's thinking immediately focuses on how to do the work, rather than first addressing what should be done and why. If you start with a predetermined solution, it's easy to gloss over more innovative approaches. Granted, best practices can jog your thoughts and maybe even inspire you. But one company's best practice can too easily become another company's sunk cost.

ACTION PLAN: Recognize that a company's best practices work in the context of its business processes, culture, systems, and people. Plucking a best practice and trying to graft it onto another organization will produce unpredictable results. Before you do so, try to anticipate possible pitfalls and challenges and how they might be circumvented by modifying the best practice. Consider best practices inspiration and food for thought—not a ready-to-use plan.

EVEN BETTER: Change takes root more effectively when it comes from within, so do what you can to develop best practices internally. In fact, having best practices come down from on high usually causes resentment. Let people create their own solutions using their in-depth knowledge of the company's customers, suppliers, employees, and processes. That will result in ownership of the ideas and determination to get results.

RULE TWO HUNDRED FORTY-FIVE
LEARN THE CORPORATE CULTURE AND MAKE IT YOUR OWN

There's a certain ambience to every organization. Maybe some are more cheerfully chaotic, whereas others are more buttoned-down and straight-laced, wherein popping your head inside an associate's office without a prior appointment just isn't done. You need to conform to what these unspoken rules and customs say is "the way things are done around here," or you'll risk rubbing people the wrong way.

WHAT IT MEANS: What is corporate culture? Essentially, it's the personality of an organization, and it guides how employees think, act, and feel. *Corporate culture* is a broad term used to define the unique personality or character of a particular company or organization, and includes such elements as core values and beliefs, corporate ethics, and rules of behavior. Corporate culture can be expressed in the company's mission statement and other communications, in the architectural style or interior décor of offices, by what people wear to work, by how people address each other, and in the titles given to various employees. Is the environment loose or authoritarian? airy or cluttered? openly competitive or more collaborative? Corporate culture is certainly something that you, as a manager or boss, can influence, but it's never something that you can fully control, and it can't be easily or rapidly changed.

ACTION PLAN: Try to gain a better understanding of your corporate culture so you can work more effectively within it. Ask yourself:

What ten words best describe your company?

How would you describe your company's spirit, personality, and morale?

What is really important—that is, what behaviors get rewarded?

What are some of the "unwritten rules"?

How would you compare this company with other places you've worked?

Get feedback on these questions from other members of your team. The emerging consensus will give you a better read on your company's personality and will indicate areas that might be impeding change and innovation.

EVEN BETTER: Make sure to communicate your corporate culture to job candidates and new hires. By knowing the "real deal" up front, they will be able to make a more informed decision—and you are apt to attract people who are more likely to fit your culture. That, in turn, can lead to greater employee retention and higher morale—both of which can boost your bottom line.

RULE TWO HUNDRED FORTY-SIX
DON'T WAIT UNTIL YOU'RE HIRED TO BEGIN YOUR NEXT JOB

It's one thing to claim you're the one to hire. Anyone can do that. But can you prove it? Showing that you've taken the time to research and constructively address the company's problems and challenges can dramatically propel you to the top of the list. It shows initiative, resourcefulness, and an ability to do the job—even before Day One!

WHAT IT MEANS: According to Nick Corcodilos, author of *Ask the Headhunter*, "To get a hiring manager's attention, you should become an expert in his business, understand the work he needs done, and find out how he would want you to do it. Then walk in and prove to him that you're going to make his business more successful." Say you're looking for a sales job. You can research your target company and create a marketing plan, bring qualified leads to the interview, research the competition to uncover selling opportunities—or all of the above. What if you want a job in IT or any other field? Research your target company's products and customers on their Web site, then write a list of possible improvements based on what you find and what you've done for other companies (or what you learned in school). Want to prove your talent as a writer or editor? Bring writing samples to the interview, and write up a special report about your target employer based on what your research tells you.

ACTION PLAN: Network your way into the company and ask employees what their biggest frustrations are. You will get an earful of answers. Now, do you think it *might* get a hiring manager's attention if you were to call and say, "I've just interviewed five people in your IT department and boiled their comments down to three major problems facing your company. I've solved each of these problems before, and I'd welcome the opportunity to do the same for you. Could I meet with you for a cup of coffee tomorrow morning and show you my findings?"

EVEN BETTER: What if you don't know anyone at Company X? Doesn't matter. The strategy still works—you just have to change your tactics. Web sites like *www.LinkedIn.com* let you make contact with people at almost any company, in almost any industry. And LinkedIn.com is absolutely free. In fact, you can't afford *not* to use it. With the right mix of research, preparation, and gumption, you can differentiate yourself from the rest of the pack in a dynamically distinctive—and impressive—way.

RULE TWO HUNDRED FORTY-SEVEN
Keep Your Secrets Secret

When negotiating agreements with other parties or companies, there may be times when sensitive company information will be shared. In fact, it is often impossible to seal a deal with another party without divulging some proprietary information. One way to protect yourself and your company from the improper release of this important information is to enter into a nondisclosure agreement before beginning the negotiations. You can make such an agreement a requirement, if you wish.

WHAT IT MEANS: A strong nondisclosure agreement is especially critical to any company with "trade secrets" that it wants to protect. Information that can be protected by an agreement includes trade secrets, employee data, customer lists, proprietary processes, and corporate business plans. Your company should insist that all employees agree, in writing, not to disclose or use the company's proprietary information without prior authorization from a specified party. The writing should stress that this obligation does not end with the employee's termination, whether voluntary or involuntary. The chances are that you won't have to go to court to enforce these contracts, but they serve to put employees and prospective business partners on notice that you are serious about keeping your proprietary information confidential. Make such agreements a condition for hiring or working with all employees, consultants, and independent contractors, as well as any business partner (ad agency, suppliers, distributors, etc.) who may be privy to your trade secrets.

ACTION PLAN: Have your lawyer draft a boilerplate nondisclosure form and gain the benefit of his or her professional expertise in this area. Alternatively, many sample nondisclosure forms can be found on the Internet—but you might still wish to seek legal counsel to modify the form to your particular needs.

EVEN BETTER: In the absence of nondisclosure or noncompete agreements, departing employees are basically free to compete against their former employer. Although some states do have laws that prohibit the disclosure of company secrets, enforcement and legal recourse can be challenging without an agreement. You should seek to obtain this additional confidentiality safeguard from senior managers or anyone in a position to potentially use your own trade secrets or other proprietary information against you.

RULE TWO HUNDRED FORTY-EIGHT
KEEP YOUR CORPORATE RECORDS UP TO DATE

If your business is a corporation, you have a corporate minutes book, officers, resolutions, and a corporate seal. This legal paraphernalia can be ignored most of the time, but there will be times you need it (bank loans, leasing and equipment contracts, share transactions, formally authorizing a profit-sharing plan, a change in corporate officers, etc.). For those times, you will want everything accessible and in order.

WHAT IT MEANS: Whatever form a business takes, the owners must make sure it is properly organized, with updated records of stock issuance or ownership and so forth. Formal corporate records must be kept up to date to avoid the owners' potential liability to the company's creditors. These records include documentation of annual meetings, board meetings, resolutions, and election of officers. In addition, state agencies require periodic filings of corporate information. Beyond formal organizational records, the business should properly document any agreements between the owners concerning the way the business will be run. For a corporation, this could include shareholder agreements. Owners may also want agreements covering possible problem areas, for example, buyout plans, succession, or sale of an owner's interest to other parties. Old agreements may need updating.

ACTION PLAN: Pick an annual date, perhaps with your lawyer, to review your corporate records and determine what changes might be necessary. Also, if being well organized is not one of your primary skills, delegate to someone else the responsibility of storing and securing your corporate records.

EVEN BETTER: Discuss with your lawyer whether certain imminent or otherwise planned activities (partnerships, acquisitions, agreements, stock transactions, adopting a company health-care plan, etc.) should be authorized with a formal corporate resolution. Gain a better understanding of what needs to be done (and when) to keep your records current.

A Streamlined Business Moves Faster ... and Makes More

Chances are, you've heard the phrase "A penny saved is a penny earned." In the business world, nothing is closer to the truth. Whether you're a start-up or a global conglomerate, your resources—people, time, and money—are limited. No company can really afford to waste money indefinitely, and for most companies in the real world, "indefinitely" can come pretty darn soon. The dollar that you save today could keep your company afloat (and your prices more competitive) tomorrow.

WHAT IT MEANS: Unless they are continually monitored, costs have a way of creeping out of control faster than a kudzu vine. It's not the only thing you need to do to keep your business fiscally fit, but it is right up there at the top. And as an owner or top manager, people will take their cue from you—so lead by example. These days, it's easier than ever to hunt for bargains on the Web. Do it. Challenge your suppliers to remain cost-competitive—or find new suppliers. Outsource what you can. The key to staying competitive, as always, is to do it faster, better, and cheaper. Pinching pennies—here, there, and everywhere—can really add up. As for exactly where to reduce costs, seek and ye shall find—so seek persistently and enlist your troops!

ACTION PLAN: If you have an accounting department, regularly conduct cost-control audits, and make sure you understand the findings and recommendations. Decide what processes and policies you can implement that can support your cost-cutting objectives.

EVEN BETTER: Make sure that managers receive regular reports that indicate the costs their departments have incurred (benchmarked against budget), and make cost control a high-priority criterion of their performance review. Also, consider other ways of recognizing and rewarding exemplary cost-cutting ideas and achievements.

RULE TWO HUNDRED FIFTY
It's OK to say, "I don't know"

Do not—repeat, *do not* fake your way through an evasive, oblique, or indirect attempt at an answer. You will, at times be tempted to do so. You may, on occasion, even get away with it—but the potential risk to your reputation and integrity is just not worth it.

WHAT IT MEANS: How many times have you been in a meeting with someone who felt compelled to contribute, even though he obviously had no idea what he was talking about? In those circumstances, silence is golden. Confident people know their strengths and weaknesses, and they don't try to B.S. you. You are not expected to know the answer to everything. Smart people simply say "I don't know"—and go get an answer. Sure, it can be embarrassing to admit ignorance—especially in front of a group or especially when you're the so-called "expert" who's giving the presentation, but you know what?

Most of the time, others will respect you for it. When you try to kid yourself or others, you always get a bad result. The truth always surfaces. A lot of people in business these days trap themselves by putting on a facade. As Warren Buffet's father once told him, "It takes you thirty years to build a reputation, but you can ruin it in thirty seconds."

ACTION PLAN: The next time you don't know something, in any work-related situation, admit simply (and without excuses or embellishment) that you don't know the answer. Make a note of the question. Quickly find out the answer to the question.

And promptly follow up with an email or call to the questioner.

EVEN BETTER: Try to anticipate what questions you are likely to be asked in any meeting or presentation. Obviously, you can't anticipate everything, but the additional homework and practice will add confidence and polish. Also, it's OK to speculate or give your best guess in response to a question—but make it very clear whenever you do so.

About Steven Schragis

Before founding One Day University in 2006, Steven's career has spanned a variety of roles in education and media. He was the Founder / CEO and Publisher of the Carol Publishing Group, parent company of Citadel Press, University Books, Birch Lane Press and Lyle Stuart. His companies published nearly 2000 books including 12 national NY Times bestsellers—two that reached #1 in over a dozen countries. Steven was Co-Founder and Publishing Director of *Spy Magazine*, one of the most influential media properties in recent decades, as well as Marketing Director of Reed Business Information, one of the world's largest publishers of trade magazines and business information. He was also the Marketing Director of the Doral Hotel Corporation.

As an attorney admitted to practice in New York and Florida, and has taught intellectual property law and marketing classes at New York University, the University of Chicago, and Harvard Law School. He has been profiled in *Forbes, New York Magazine, The Wall Street Journal* and on *PBS and NPR* in connection with his innovations in continuing education

ABOUT RICK FRISHMAN

Rick Frishman, publisher at Morgan James Publishing in New York and founder of Planned Television Arts (now called Media Connect), has been one of the leading book publicists in America for over 36 years. Rick works with many of the top book editors, literary agents, and publishers in America, including Simon and Schuster, Random House, Wiley, Harper Collins, Pocket Books, Penguin Group, and Hyperion Books. He has worked with bestselling authors such as Mitch Albom, Bill Moyers, Stephen King, Caroline Kennedy, Howard Stern, President Jimmy Carter, Mark Victor Hansen, Nelson DeMille, John Grisham, Hugh Downs, Henry Kissinger, Jack Canfield, Alan Deshowitz, Arnold Palmer, and Harvey Mackay.

Morgan James Publishing publishes fiction and nonfiction books and by authors with a platform who believe in giving back. Morgan James gives a portion of every book sold to Habitat for Humanity.

Rick has also appeared on hundreds of radio shows and more than a dozen TV shows nationwide, including *Oprah* and Bloomberg TV. He has also been featured in the *New York Times, Wall Street Journal, Associated Press, Selling Power Magazine, New York Post*, and scores of other publications.

He has appeared on stage with notables such as The Dalai Lama, Sir Richard Branson, T. Harv Eker, Jack Canfield, Mark Victor Hansen, Tony Hsieh, David Bach, Brian Tracy, and Brendon Burchard.

Rick is the coauthor of thirteen books, including national bestsellers *Guerrilla Publicity, Networking Magic, Where's Your Wow?, Guerrilla Marketing for Writers,* and *Show Me About Book Publishing.* "250 Rules of Business " is Rick's *thirteenth* book.

Rick has a BFA in acting and directing and a BS in communications from Ithaca College. He is a sought-after lecturer on publishing and public relations and a member of PRSA and the National Speakers Association.

Rick and his wife Robbi live in Long Island, New York with their two Havanese puppies, Cody and Cooper. They have three children: Adam, Rachel, and Stephanie.

Go to http://www.rickfrishman.com for more information and to get Rick's *Million Dollar Rolodex*. Email rick@rickfrishman.com.

BONUS INFORMATION

Printed in the USA
CPSIA information can be obtained
at www.ICGtesting.com
JSHW022218140824
68134JS00018B/1125